I0883962

The Chalmers Lecture

FREE CHURCH PRINCIPLES

The Chalmers Lecture

FREE CHURCH PRINCIPLES

BY

THE REV. WILLIAM WILSON, D.D.

Wipf and Stock Publishers
EUGENE, OREGON

Wipf and Stock Publishers
199 West 8th Avenue, Suite 3
Eugene, Oregon 97401

Free Church Principles
The Chalmers Lecture
By Wilson, William
ISBN: 1-59244-419-9
Publication date 11/12/2003
Previously published by MacNiven & Wallace, 1887

EXTRACT FROM THE DEED INSTITUTING THE CHALMERS LECTURESHIP. (The Deed being dated 26th May 1880.)

"I, ROBERT MACFIE, Esq. of Airds and Oban, considering that I feel deeply interested in the maintenance of the principles of the Free Church of Scotland, have transferred . . . the sum of £5000 sterling for the purpose of founding a Lectureship in memory of the late THOMAS CHALMERS, D.D., LL.D., under the following conditions: namely—1. The Lectureship shall . . . be called *The Chalmers Lectureship*; 2. The Lecturer shall hold the appointment for four years, and shall be entitled . . . to one-half of the income. . . . 3. The subject shall be 'Headship of Christ over His Church, and its independent Spiritual Jurisdiction;' 4. The Lecturer shall be bound to deliver publicly a Course of not fewer than six Lectures . . . in Edinburgh, in Glasgow, and in Aberdeen; 5. The Lecturer shall be bound, within a year, to print and publish at his own risk not fewer than 1500 copies . . . and deposit three copies in the libraries of the Free Church Colleges; 6. One-half of the balance of the income . . . shall be laid out in furnishing with a copy all the Ministers and Missionaries of the Free Church . . . . . ."

CONTENTS.

LECTURE I.

CHRIST, HEAD OVER ALL THINGS.

It seems desirable, if indeed it may not be considered as necessary, that before proceeding directly to consider the theme of this Lectureship, something should be said of the dominion over all things with which Christ has been invested as Mediator. This dominion is different from that which He possesses and exercises as God, and different also from that which He exercises in and over the Church. All this is made clear enough from what is stated in the Epistle to the Ephesians, "The God of our Lord Jesus Christ, the Father of glory . . . raised Him from the dead, and set Him at His own right hand in the heavenly places, far above all principality and power, and might, and dominion, and every name that is named, not only in this world, but also in that which is to come; and hath put all things under His feet, and gave Him to be the

Head over all things to the Church, which is His body, the fulness of Him that filleth all in all" (Eph. i. 17, 20-23). Statements of substantially the same import are made in many other passages of Scripture. His dominion as Mediator is said to be given Him as the reward and fruit of His humiliation, and His obedience unto death. His dominion as God is not derived or delegated. But it is given Him as Mediator, to be the Head over all things to the Church, which is His body. He is the Head of the Church. He is Head over all things to the Church. There is thus a threefold relation which He sustains.

First. As God, He is over all things, "For by Him were all things created that are in heaven, and that are in earth, visible and invisible, whether they be thrones, or dominions, or principalities, or powers; all things were created by Him, and for Him; and He is before all things, and by Him all things consist" (Col. i. 16, 17). He is the eternal Logos by whom the unseen God expresses and manifests Himself; and "all things were made by Him; and without Him was not anything made that was made" (John i. 3). Therefore universal power and authority belong to Him inherently and without delegation, as the Eternal Son of the Father, the Maker and Sustainer of all things.

Second. But there is also a dominion which is said to be given to Him as the Son of Man, the Word made flesh—a delegated authority, with which He is invested as Mediator, and which He exercises for the complete accomplishment of those ends for which "He humbled Himself, and became obedient unto death, even the death of the cross" (Phil. ii. 8). It is therefore that "God has highly exalted Him, and given Him a name which is above every name" (Phil. ii. 9). Christ Himself said, after He was revealed as the conqueror of death by His resurrection from the dead, "All power is given unto Me in heaven and in earth" (Matt. xxviii. 18); and in virtue of the gift to Him of this power, He commissioned His apostles to go and make disciples of all nations. And on the day of Pentecost Peter declared to the assembled Jews, "Let all the house of Israel know assuredly that God hath made that same Jesus, whom ye have crucified, both Lord and Christ" (Acts ii. 36).

Third. But the relation in which He stands to

the Church is more intimate and more vital than that of ruler and subject. He is not only its Lord, but its Head. The Church is His body. He is one with it. He has identified Himself with it. In His death it suffered the penalty of the broken law, and it is raised up together with Him, and is made to sit together with Him in the heavenly places. It lives in Him, and He lives in it. It is complete in Him, and it is His fulness. Of it He says in His prayer to the Father: "The glory which Thou gavest Me I have given them; that they may be one, even as We are one: I in them, and Thou in Me, that they may be made perfect in one (John xvii. 22, 23).

It is with the second of these topics we shall take to do in the present Lecture—namely, the Dominion of Christ over all things as Mediator. To this exalted position He was raised when His work of humiliation was perfected, and when He was able to say of it—It is finished. This does not imply that He was denuded of His universal supremacy as the Creator and Lord of all. This supremacy is implied in His Godhead, and is inherent in Him as Divine. But His investiture with all power in heaven and in earth as Mediator was a solemn delegation to Him of a new exercise of power, and a declaration to all intelligences that it would be directed to the accomplishment of the ends of His humiliation. The fact, however, that He was raised to supreme power as the reward of His finished work does not preclude the idea that from the commencement of human history—at least from the entrance of sin into the world—He was ordained as Mediator, and performed all the acts of mediation. There never has been but one way of saving sinners. And just as the efficacy of His atoning sacrifice reaches back to the institution of sacrifice, and the accepted offering of Abel, so His mediatorial sovereignty was exercised in the salvation of His people : "In subduing them to Himself, and in restraining and conquering all His and their enemies." In the councils of eternity He was ordained as Mediator, but it was only when His redeeming work was done that He was conspicuously and formally invested with this sovereignty, and all things were put under His feet.

His lordship is universal, but He reigns as a

Priest, and in virtue of that atoning sacrifice, in which "mercy and truth met together; righteousness and peace kissed each other" (Ps. lxxxv. 10). In vision, on the Isle of Patmos, John beheld Him standing in the midst of the throne, and of the four living creatures, and in the midst of the elders, like a Lamb as it had been slain; and to Him it was given to open the sealed book of the Divine purposes, and to carry them into full accomplishment in the salvation of His people. They are represented as singing a new song to Him, because He has redeemed them by His blood. And the angels, joining the celestial choir, sang with a loud voice, "Worthy is the Lamb that was slain to receive power, and riches, and wisdom, and strength, and honour, and glory, and blessing. And every creature which is in heaven and on earth, and under the earth, and such as are in the sea, and all that are in them, are heard saying, Blessing, and honour, and glory, and power be unto Him that sitteth upon the throne, and unto the Lamb for ever and ever" (Rev. v.) This ascription of power and glory to Him as the Lamb indicates that the supremacy to which He has been exalted is to subserve the ends for which He gave Himself a sacrifice and offering without spot unto God. And He intimates to His apostles that all power in heaven and in earth is given to Him as the formal reason of His commission to them to go and make disciples of all nations. But for His possession of this power, nothing could have been more vain and futile than such a charge. What they were enjoined to do was so manifestly impossible to them, that they could not otherwise have been induced to undertake it. What hope could they have of changing the attitude of a single soul towards Christ? His own countrymen, only a few weeks before, had with one voice demanded that He should be crucified, and the Roman Governor had consented to doom Him to the most shameful death as a malefactor. There was no evidence anywhere of a friendly disposition towards Him, and He had Himself forewarned them that they would be hated of all men for His name's sake. What could they do to remove this rooted and universal enmity? What inducement could they present to any man to become a disciple of the Crucified? And yet they received the injunction, and accepted its responsibilities, in the faith that all power was His, and notwithstanding of their manifest disqualification for the great work they were called to do. They had no position of influence in the world: they were not learned doctors, skilled in the arts of persuasion; they were ignorant and unlearned men. But they had confidence in the power which He declared had been given to Him. They had already, indeed, some experience of its reality when they had been sent forth by Him on a brief mission to their own countrymen, and had found that they could in His name cast out devils and heal diseases. They received the charge given to them in the belief that the power by which He is able to subdue all things to Himself would accompany them, and be in them, in the prosecution of their gigantic mission.

But in order to their success, and in order always to the preservation and extension of the Church, it is necessary that Christ should possess and exercise this power. Hence the universal dominion over all things which has been given Him. It is a power necessary for the accomplishment of God's gracious purposes towards the children of men, and in the exercise of which Christ now lives and reigns.

All power in heaven has been given to Him for this end. In evidence of this, the Holy Ghost was sent by Him to abide with men on the earth —a perpetual witness of the glory and dominion of the risen Lord. On the day of Pentecost He descended upon the disciples in the form of cloven tongues of fire, and endowed them with all needed gifts, not only enabling them to speak in various tongues, but to speak with efficacy for the conversion of sinners. To the assembled multitude, filled with amazement at what they saw and heard, Peter testified that "God had raised up Jesus whom they had crucified." "Therefore," he added, "being by the right hand of God exalted, and having received of the Father the promise of the Holy Ghost, He hath shed forth this which ye now see and hear" (Acts ii. 33). Nor was this sending forth of the Divine Spirit in vain, for on that day there were added to the Church about three thousand souls, who continued steadfastly in the apostles' doctrine and fellowship. Such a result was fitted to inspire the apostles with confident hope as to the result of their mission, for nowhere in the world could they be brought face to face with more hardened and bitter enemies of Christ than in the heart of Jerusalem. Peter spoke to them as men who had taken Christ, and by wicked hands had crucified and slain Him. Thus, and so early, was fulfilled the word which the Lord had spoken to His disciples on the evening of the Passover, to quiet the trouble and fear which were oppressing them : "It is expedient for you that I go away : for if I go not away, the Comforter will not come unto you ; but if I depart, I will send Him unto you. And when He is come, He will reprove the world of sin, and of righteousness, and of judgment" (John xvi. 7, 8). "He shall glorify Me : for He shall receive of Mine, and shall show it unto you. All things that the Father hath are Mine" (verses 14, 15). And again, on the same occasion, He said, "He that believeth on Me, the works that I do shall he do also ; and greater works than these shall he do ; because I go unto My Father" (John xiv. 12). This word also was now verified to them, for Jesus by His personal ministry had never done such a great work as that which they now saw accomplished—a work which rendered probable the subjugation of the whole world to the obedience of Christ.

This mission of the Holy Ghost is not the only evidence of the power which Christ possesses and exercises in heaven. He employs the angels also to fulfil His pleasure as agents, in guarding the welfare of those whom He has redeemed, and in fulfilling His gracious purpose regarding them. They are all employed as "ministering spirits, sent forth to minister for them who shall be heirs of salvation" (Heb. i. 14). We have no knowledge, indeed, of the way in which these spirits fulfil their ministry, and what acts of service they perform on behalf of Christ's people; but we are assured that they are employed in some beneficent way in defending their interests and promoting their welfare. The heirs of salvation are their special charge.

But it is not in heaven only that power has been given to Christ. All power in earth is also given to Him. He has power not only over men, but over all agencies and things that can influence them, and affect their character and conduct. His people are in such a position that they are called to wrestle not against flesh and blood only, but "against principalities, against powers, against the rulers of the darkness of this world, against spiritual wickedness in high places" (Eph. vi. 12).

And therefore Christ has power over these spirits of darkness to restrain their malice, so that they shall not lead His people captive at their will. In the exercise of His supreme wisdom indeed He does not prevent them being exposed to the wiles of the devil, for they need trial and discipline of all kinds to purify and strengthen them. But evil spirits are made His unwilling agents in making perfect that which concerneth them. Peter was made able to strengthen his brethren, and became the prince and chief of the apostles, by his bitter experience of that temptation by which he was induced to deny his Lord. Out of weakness he was made strong, and was henceforth victorious over all shrinking fear.

Christ has also supreme dominion over all nations and their rulers. They are not indeed kingdoms of Christ, but they are placed in subjection under Him, so that He can render them subservient to the ends of His mediatorial authority, and to the interests of His redeemed people. The Scripture testimony on this subject is very abundant and specific. It is implied, indeed, in the fact of His sovereignty over all things—a sovereignty which is not only His as God, but which is given to Him as Mediator. For His dominion over all things cannot but imply nations and their rulers, which play such an important part in the history of the world, and whose movements so largely affect the condition of His people. It is implied, indeed, in the commission to His disciples to go and teach all nations. On the power given to Him as Mediator rests the warrant which His ambassadors have to penetrate into all kingdoms, and to prosecute their vocation in every nation of the world. In doing so they are not invaders of a foreign territory, and have no need to wait the slow process of negotiations with governments, or solicit permission to take up their abode in any kingdom and to deliver their testimony. The universal dominion of Christ gives them the right of access to all nations. They go armed with the authority of Him by whom kings reign and princes decree justice. These rulers exercise their authority in subordination to Him who is Head over all things. They reign by His permission, and to subserve the ends of His supreme government. His ambassadors therefore have the right of access into every kingdom, and the right to establish in it that kingdom which is righteousness and peace and joy in the Holy Ghost. They are not instructed ere they go to ask the permission of kings, or to enter into any relation with them. They are commanded simply to go and do the work assigned to them, with the view of subduing all nations to the obedience of Christ. In doing their work they are not dependent on the good will of kings, nor are they obliged to submit to their mandates, or thereby to regulate their procedure. They are strangers and foreigners in no country, for they are the subjects of Him to whom all the world belongs. Earthly potentates may indeed, and most frequently do, ignore and resist such a claim, but it is not on that account the less valid. In doing so, they disown the authority of Him who is Lord over all.

The Scripture testimony as to Christ's lordship over the nations is, as I have said, very abundant and specific. It is said of the ten kings spoken of in the book of Revelation, that they "shall make war with the Lamb, and the Lamb shall overcome them, for He is Lord of lords, and King of kings" (Rev. xvii. 14). And when He is represented as coming forth in His glorious Majesty, He is seen as having "on His vesture and on His thigh a name written, KING OF KINGS AND LORD OF LORDS" (Rev. xix. 16.) In the second psalm, which, in the sermon preached by Peter on the day of Pentecost, is said to be spoken of Christ, this honour is ascribed to Him: "Thou art My Son; this day have I begotten Thee. Ask of Me, and I shall give Thee the heathen for Thine inheritance, and the uttermost parts of the earth for Thy possession. Thou shalt break them with a rod of iron; Thou shalt dash them in pieces like a potter's vessel. Be wise now therefore, O ye kings; be instructed, ye judges of the earth. Serve the Lord with fear, and rejoice with trembling. Kiss the Son lest He be angry, and ye perish from the way, when His wrath is kindled but a little. Blessed are all they that put their trust in Him" (Ps. ii. 7-12). Surely it cannot be doubted that when kings, and state-officers such as judges, are enjoined to serve the

Lord with fear, He has a rightful claim upon their service; and it is equally clear that the Lord whom they are commanded to serve is no other than Christ. In the book of Daniel we read, "And I saw in the night-visions, and, behold, one like the Son of Man came with the clouds of heaven, and came to the Ancient of Days, and they brought Him near before Him. And there was given Him dominion, and glory, and a kingdom, that all people, nations, and languages, should serve Him: His dominion is an everlasting dominion, which shall not pass away, and His kingdom that which shall not be destroyed" (Daniel vii. 13, 14). The Son of Man is a very distinctive designation of Christ, for by this name more frequently than by any other He spoke of Himself; and the fact of the dominion being given Him, clearly indicates that He possesses it as Mediator. The dominion being over nations, moreover, sufficiently indicates that all those rulers and administrative agents, by which a nation is organised, are subject to Him, and are under obligation to serve Him. Again, in Psalm xxii. 28, which manifestly refers to Christ, it is said, "The kingdom is the Lord's; and He is

Governor among the nations." It might be tedious, and it does not seem to be necessary, to quote many other passages of Scripture indicating the same truth. This only may be added, that the frequent assertions in the New Testament, regarding the universality of His dominion, all imply that He is Lord over all earthly potentates and nations. "All things," He says, "are delivered unto Me of My Father" (Matt. xi. 27). Peter speaks of Him as Lord of all. Paul, addressing the Colossians, says, "Ye are complete in Him which is the Head of all principality and power" (Col. ii. 10). In the Epistle to the Hebrews, speaking undoubtedly of Christ and in reference to Psalm viii., it is said, "Thou madest Him a little lower than the angels; Thou crownedst Him with glory and honour, and didst set Him over the works of Thy hands: Thou hast put all things in subjection under His feet. For in that He put all in subjection under Him, He left nothing that is not put under Him" (Hebrews ii. 7, 8.) And to the same effect, in the first Epistle to the Corinthians, it is said, "For He hath put all things under His feet. But when He saith, all things are put under Him, it is manifest that He is excepted which did put all things under Him" (1 Cor. xv. 27). That is, the one exception to the universality of Christ's dominion is God the Father.

It is so obvious that it scarcely needs to be stated, that when Christ is spoken of as Governor among the nations we must understand nations, not as consisting of the aggregate of the individuals who compose them, but as organisations —as bodies acting in unison, by whatever administrations they may be compacted. If they are without laws, and subject to the arbitrary will of one ruler, Christ is the Lord of that ruler, who is responsible to Him in his acts of government, and who will be judged by Him. If the government is of a mixed character, and is regulated by laws, and has judges and legislators, and various forms of administration, those who frame the laws, and those who execute them, are alike subject to Christ, and should have respect to His supreme authority, ruling in the fear of the Lord. Recognising His supreme authority they are under obligation, not as individuals merely, but in their capacity as rulers, to have respect to His will, and to legislate and act under a sense of responsibility to Him, and to take heed not to traverse His law. He holds them responsible, and judges them, and deals with them as bound to serve Him.

Looking to the history of nations, it does seem somewhat extravagant to say that they are subject to Christ as Mediator, who, as such, rules over them in subordination to the welfare of His people. For almost universally worldly potentates have been the enemies of the Church of Christ. They have opposed and endeavoured to exterminate it, or to make it subservient to their carnal ambition. It was so in the person of Jesus Himself, as indicated in the prophetic psalm: "The kings of the earth set themselves, and the rulers take counsel together, against the Lord, and against His Anointed" (Ps. ii. 2). And it has been so in almost all lands in which the Church has been planted, from the age of Nero down to the present day. And when the red hand of persecution has been stayed, and the rulers of this world have become the friends and patrons of the Church, the results have not been more favourable to its interests. Their embrace has been as deadly as their hostility; they have enslaved it, and made it the instrument of promoting the ends of their carnal policy. They cannot endure a pure Church, walking in the light of God's truth, and acting in conformity with His will. Of this we have had in our own land a large experience, from the time of the Reformation till the present day.

But if all this be so—if so generally the rulers of nations have shown themselves to be either the oppressors or the corrupters of the Church, or its bloody persecutors—how can it be said with truth that the Mediator is Lord over them, and uses them in promoting the high ends of His mediatorial office? Have the rulers of this world really been made subservient to the interests of Christ's cause and people? Does not the history of Christianity prove the very reverse? Looking superficially at this matter, one would be disposed to say, that in reference to the interests of the Church the action of State rulers has been disastrous. And yet, when we examine the question more profoundly, may it not after all be true that their hostility or their oppression has been among the "all things" that work together for good to them who love God? Who is there that can fathom the depths of Divine Providence? Who can tell what greater corruptions might not have invaded the Church, but for the chastening hand of persecution! Are we in a position to estimate what sort of discipline Christ's people need to make them "meet for the inheritance of the saints in light?" Has not the Lord, in the recent experience of His people in this country, been teaching us what manifold and rich blessings have resulted from what His people regarded with dread, as pregnant with disaster? Has not the oppressive hand of our rulers brought us into a position of greater enlargement and liberty? Yea, did not the devices of the wicked in crucifying the Lord of Glory issue in the salvation of the world?

> "God moves in a mysterious way
> His wonders to perform;
> He plants His footsteps in the sea,
> And rides upon the storm.
>
> "Ye fearful saints, fresh courage take;
> The clouds ye so much dread
> Are big with mercy, and shall break
> In blessings on your head."

Our limits do not permit us to expatiate further on this particular theme, and we proceed accordingly to notice, in respect to Christ's dominion, that it extends over all the relations of human society, as well as over rulers and subjects. It embraces masters and servants, husbands and wives, parents and children, brothers and sisters. Christ rules in all these relations, and asserts the right of instructing those who sustain them in the duties which they involve: "Servants, be obedient to them that are your masters according to the flesh; . . . not with eye-service, as men-pleasers, but as the servants of Christ." "And, ye masters, do the same thing unto them, forbearing threatening." "Husbands, love your wives, even as Christ also loved the Church." "Wives, submit yourselves unto your own husbands, as unto the Lord." "Children, obey your parents in the Lord." "And, ye fathers, provoke not your children to wrath." (Eph. v. vi.) "Be kindly affectioned one to another with brotherly love, in honour preferring one another" (Rom. xii. 10). Such are some of the injunctions which the Lord has given affecting our domestic and social relations; and all of them imply that He has rightful authority in determining the obligations which are involved in them. These relations moreover, and especially those of the domestic circle, are more influential than any others in this world in moulding the character and in determining the conduct of men; and from this alone we might infer that Christ should have authority over them—that He might use them on behalf of His people for making perfect that which concerneth them.

But it is not only over all intelligent beings that Christ has been made the Head. His lordship is, in the most comprehensive sense, universal. There is not anything that is not put under Him. The beasts of the field, and the fowls of the air, and the fish of the sea, are all under His dominion. It embraces the whole creation, animate and inanimate. The sun, and moon, and stars are under His sway. The winds and waves obey Him. It is said of Him in Psalm viii., which by inspired authority is applied to Christ, "Thou madest Him to have dominion over the works of Thy hands; Thou hast put all things under His feet, all sheep and oxen, yea, and the beasts of the field, the fowls of the air, and the fish of the sea, and whatsoever passeth through the paths of the sea."

Even in the days of His humiliation, and in anticipation of His exaltation and glory, He made this authoritative power manifest. The stormy wind was stilled at His bidding, and He walked upon the waves of the sea. In subjection to His will, the fishermen of Galilee, whom He made fishers of men, had their net filled. And in Old Testament times a path was made by Him through the Red Sea for the ransomed of the Lord to pass through, and the waters of Jordan stood together as a heap. By Him the mouths of lions were stopped, and the violence of fire was quenched to save His persecuted saints. He has power given Him over all noxious things, so that they shall not do His people harm. He has power also to execute judgment, whereby He brings to nought the devices of the wicked. He brings down the mighty from their high places, and withers the arm of the oppressor. In obedience to His will the earth opened her mouth, and swallowed up Korah and all his company; and by slow though sure processes the nations and kingdoms perish, which raise their heads in proud rebellion against Him.

It is necessary always to keep in view that

this universal dominion is given to Christ as Mediator on behalf of the Church. He is made Head over all things to the Church, which is His body and His fulness. It was in His union with the Church, and as Mediator, that He was humbled and became obedient unto death ; and it is in the same capacity that He is exalted. He died as bearing the burden of His people's sins ; it is as having met and satisfied all claims against them that all things are now put under His feet. The Church therefore has no less an interest in His exaltation and power, than she has in His humiliation and death. On her behalf He died, and it is on her behalf that He now lives and reigns. His dominion over all things is necessary for bringing His people into that state of perfection to which it is His will to raise them, that they may be presented before God a glorious Church, not having spot or wrinkle, or any such thing. He came in humiliation, in the likeness of sinful flesh, made in all points like unto His brethren, with whom He consented to be identified, not on His own account, to take the sting from death, by taking away sin, and to contend against and overcome devils and wicked men. It was on behalf of His Church that He disarmed and defeated all His and their enemies. And now, neither is it on His own account that He is made Head over all things. He wields the sceptre and wears the crown for them. All that is His becomes theirs. It is they who need the exercise of His power over all, and it is they who experience the blessed deliverance which it brings. They sustain manifold relations to the creation in the midst of which they live and act—relations which more or less directly and powerfully affect them. Nothing is so remote as to have no influence on their well-being. Agencies, visible and invisible, are constantly operating upon them, the nature and power of which they are not able even fully to comprehend. They are appointed to live for a longer or shorter time exposed to these influences, and are not able to direct their own steps, and to defend themselves. The very air they breathe, the various atmospheric changes around them, the revolution of the heavenly bodies, the meat and drink by which they are sustained, the employments in which they are engaged,—all these operate through the body upon their inner nature, and insensibly affect the interests of their immortal souls, bracing them to greater vigour and healthfulness, or blunting their perceptions, and incapacitating them for discharging aright the obligations which rest upon them. The society in which they live, their intercourse with other men, the fellowship and example of those with whom they associate, the ties which unite them in families, still more directly and powerfully influence their minds for good or for evil. And besides all this, they are encompassed with an invisible agency of principalities and powers, of whose presence they are unconscious, and who obtain access to the very sources of thought and emotion, seeking with all subtlety to assert their sway over their mind and heart, and make them obedient to their behests. He therefore, who is to be the Defender and Redeemer of the Church, must be Head over all these, and have control over men and devils, and over all the visible creation. He who has usurped the dominion of this world, the prince of the power of the air, the spirit that now worketh in the children of disobedience, makes use of everything in the world to entice men from the love and service of

God, and to minister to the lust of the flesh, and the lust of the eye, and the pride of life; and He who would counteract such an agent as this, and deliver those who are under his sway, must have power over all these instruments of temptation, that He may convert them to the uses for which they were designed, and adapt them to the service of His people, again transforming this visible world into a fair temple in which the glory of God is manifested; so that, whatsoever appeals it makes to the heart and understanding, and whatsoever it presents to the eye and ear, shall continually bear witness for God, and bind the soul in willing and devoted and loving obedience to Him. And this is the security which the people of God have, not only that Christ died, and took away sin by the sacrifice of Himself, but that He is alive and liveth for evermore, and hath the keys of hell and of death. It is as Head over all things that He has been given to the Church.

If therefore I am a believer—if I have committed myself into Christ's hands, and am looking to Him as all my salvation and all my desire, I know that all things will work together for my good, for they are all under His feet, and under the direction and control of Him who loved me and gave Himself for me. Along whatever path He may lead me—whatever obstacles may oppose me—whatever influences may operate upon me, it is He who so loves me that is employing all agents and experiences for the restoration of my soul, and for conforming me to His own image. He alone, who is Head over all things, can keep me safe and make me perfect. For this very end He has received universal power, and I may rest assured that His power will be so exercised. In the world I am exposed to the same adversaries against which, in the days of His humiliation, He was called to contend. He was tempted in all points as I am, and has laid Himself alongside of me in all my experiences, and has proved His strength against my adversaries and subdued them, and has been made Head over them, so as to constrain them to serve His purposes. It may be through much painful discipline that His high purpose will be accomplished in me, but I know that He cannot fail in it, for every agent in it, animate and inanimate, is at His disposal, and that He uses them all in His gracious ministry to the Church. There may be apparent victories of evil in my experience, short-lived and vain triumphs achieved by my adversaries in order that the power and riches of His grace may be made more manifest; but just as He, in submitting to death, conquered it, so will it be in the experience of His people. The victories of evil over them, while proving their weakness, will also call forth a higher exercise of His gracious power, and make more manifest His patient love; and in committing myself unreservedly and entirely to Him, He will perfect that which concerneth me. In the exercise of His manifold wisdom and infinite love, the world, and life, and death, and things present, and things to come, will be made subservient to my highest interests, and ripen me for the glory which is to be revealed, and for my fellowship with Him on His throne.

And if all this appear to any Christian to be incredible—if, looking to the history of the Church at large, and his own experience of the trials to which he has been subjected, he finds it very hard to believe it, this is partly due, no doubt, to the inscrutable mysteries of Providence, but still more to his inadequate apprehension of the training and discipline he needs, in order that he should become what the Lord would have him to be. From the days of Job downwards, in the succeeding ages, men have endeavoured in vain to penetrate the clouds and darkness around the throne of God, and to know His ways, only a small part of which we see. We must live in faith, for we cannot in this region of contemplation walk by sight. We can see indeed in part, and are able to interpret some of His dealings; but it is on His Word our main confidence must rest, in assuring ourselves that all things work together for good to them that love God. I may not be able to apprehend why some apparently disastrous event has befallen me, nor what special purpose it serves in advancing my highest interests—much less may I be able to apprehend the whole course of Divine Providence in reference to the Church at large, or to see why He should have dealt with it as He has done, and not otherwise; but when I consider the course of my own life, and examine my own heart, I may perceive that my sins and infirmities are such as require a very wise and varied, and it may be very severe, discipline, to make me such as the Lord would have me to be. We may be able to attain no other or higher position than that reached by Job in saying, "Though He slay me, yet will I trust in Him."

LECTURE II.

CHRIST THE HEAD OF THE CHURCH.

IN our previous lecture we were engaged in contemplating Christ the Mediator as Head over all things. In the present lecture we propose to contemplate Him as the Head of the Church. The Church is spoken of as His body—the body of which He is the Head. This indicates a very close and vital relationship between Christ and the Church. They are represented as one corporation, having one life. The relationship spoken of is that of the Head to the members of the body, and implies that action in the members is regulated by the Head, and is obedient to its influence; that, apart from it, the members have no life; and that as they are all united to the Head, so they are all mutually united to each other. The Church and Christ are one organism.

The same truth is presented in another form

when Christ speaks of Himself as the true vine, and represents His disciples as branches of it, dependent for their vitality and fruitfulness on their connection with the stem. "I am the true vine," He says, "ye are the branches; without Me ye can do nothing" (John xv. 5). Paul states this in a very emphatic way when he says, "I am crucified with Christ: nevertheless I live; yet not I, but Christ liveth in me" (Gal. ii. 20); thus identifying Himself with Christ, both in His death and in His victory over death. He knew Him in the fellowship of His sufferings, and in the power of His resurrection. Nor does he aver this as anything peculiar to himself. Such union with Christ is realised by all true believers. It is this which delivers them from the fear of death, and from the bondage of the law. It is the liberty into which he invited the Galatian Church to enter; and his prayer on behalf of the Church at Ephesus was, that Christ might dwell in their hearts by faith.

But nothing is more certain than that this is not the experience of all the members of any church on earth. There are in every church more or fewer whose union with Christ is merely outward and formal. They form part of the organisation, but have not the vitality which indicates a real union with the Head. Hence it is necessary to distinguish between the Church as a visible organised body, and the Church as consisting only of those in whom Christ lives and moves, and which will finally be presented to Himself as a glorious Church without spot or wrinkle, or any such thing. This latter has properly been called the Invisible Church, which is the real body and fulness of Christ, partaker of His grace, and in which he lives and reigns. But it has no visible organisation. It is united to Christ by unseen bonds, and the sources of its life are not palpable to the senses. Its members cannot with absolute certainty be identified by any human discrimination. They "eat of the hidden manna, and there is given them a white stone, and in the stone a new name written, which no man knoweth saving he that receiveth it" (Rev. ii. 17). In two parables, Christ declares the fact that there are in the visible Church those who are saved and those who have no living union with Him, and that no discrimination of men can separate the one from the other. In the Parable of the

Tares and the Wheat, He warns us not to try to separate them. "Let both grow together until the harvest, lest while ye gather up the tares ye root up also the wheat with them" (Matt. xiii. 29). And the same thing is taught in the Parable of the Net, which being cast into the sea gathered of every kind; and it is not till the end of the world that the good are gathered into vessels and the bad are cast away" (Matt. xiii. 47, 48). And what is thus taught in parable is confirmed by all the facts of history. No church on earth ever consisted, exclusively, of living members of Christ's body, in whose hearts Christ dwelt by faith. In the family of Adam there was Cain as well as Abel; in that of Abraham, Ishmael as well as Isaac; in that of Isaac, Esau as well as Jacob. The seed of the flesh have always been mixed up with the seed of the promise. In the Church of Israel there were always men of uncircumcised heart. Christ may be said to have taught the fact of such admixture in the most significant way by having among His twelve chosen apostles Judas Iscariot, who betrayed Him. None of the churches planted by the apostles were entirely pure; and the Church in every age and land has contained within it sinners as well as saints—those who are in living union with Christ, and those who derive from Him no saving benefit. It is those only in whose hearts Christ dwells by faith who are identified with Him and constitute His fulness. It is this class which constitutes what is called the Invisible Church, and which, in the well-chosen words of the Westminster Confession, "consists of the whole number of the elect that have been, are, or shall be gathered into one under Christ, the Head thereof; and is the spouse, the body, the fulness of Him that filleth all in all." Some discrimination therefore is necessary in applying the statements of Scripture regarding the Church, and the relation to it which Christ sustains. For what is said of the Church invisible may not be true of the visible Church. But it is really not difficult in almost any case to determine what is exclusively pertinent to the saints of God, and what is fitly spoken of the visible, organised body of professing Christians.

But it is necessary, first of all, to define what is meant by the visible Church. In doing this I adopt, for I know no better definition than that which is given in the Westminster Confession: "The visible Church, which is also (as well as the invisible) catholic or universal, under the Gospel (not confined to one nation as before under the law), consists of all those throughout the world that profess the true religion as well as their children." It is not often, however, that the word is used in this comprehensive sense. The term, indeed, both in Hebrew and Greek, which is rendered by the word Church in its primary meaning, is applied to any assembly, whether civil or ecclesiastical, which is gathered together out of the mass of the people. It does not even imply that they shall be regularly organised. For example, the mob at Ephesus, instigated by Demetrius, the silversmith, who assaulted Paul and his companions, are designated by this term. "Some cried one thing and some another, for the assembly (church) was confused" (Acts xix. 32). The word accordingly is variously applied in Scripture, and the meaning which must be attached to it must be gathered from the circumstances in which it is employed. It is used frequently in a sense in which it can only mean the body of true believers who are saved by

Christ; as, for example, in Eph. ii. 21, 22, in which it is spoken of under the figure of a temple: "In Christ all the building, fitly framed together, groweth unto an holy temple in the Lord: in whom ye also are builded together for an habitation of God through the Spirit." And in the same Epistle we find a similar application of it: "Husbands, love your wives, even as Christ also loved the Church, and gave Himself for it; that He might sanctify and cleanse it with the washing of water by the Word, that He might present it to Himself a glorious Church, not having spot, or wrinkle, or any such thing; but that it should be holy, and without blemish" (Eph. v. 25-27). These things are manifestly spoken of the Church invisible. But the society of professing Christians, as organised and visible, is also designated by the term Church, as for instance (1 Cor. xii. 27, 28), "Now ye are the body of Christ, and members in particular. And God has set some in the Church, first, apostles; secondarily, prophets; thirdly, teachers; after that miracles, then gifts of healing, helps, governments, diversities of tongues." But however small the company of professing Christians may be in any one place, they are designated as a church. Philemon is addressed as having a church in his house. Priscilla and Aquila are also represented as having a church in their house. And in the Acts of the Apostles we are told that Paul and Barnabas, in their missionary journey, ordained them elders in every church. And in the Epistle to Titus Paul says, "For this cause left I thee in Crete, that thou shouldest set in order the things that are wanting, and ordain elders in every city, as I had appointed thee" (Titus i. 5). In these cases the Church is spoken of, not in its universal character, but as existing and organised in particular localities—as congregations of professing Christians. In places, moreover, in which it is certain there were several congregations, they are spoken of as forming one church; as, for instance, in the Church at Jerusalem, which from its numbers could not have been assembled together in one building, but were organised under one government. The meeting of church rulers, also assembled for the exercise of discipline, is spoken of as a church. (Matt. xviii. 17.)

But, amid these diverse applications of the

term, it is manifest that the same class of persons is meant. It is a profession of faith in Christ, by a body of people, which constitutes them a church ; and the visible Church consists of all those in every place who credibly make such a profession, and in which the ordinances of Christ's appointment are observed, and, with a view to this, in which officers of administration are appointed. All this is implied in the Scripture statements that have been quoted or referred to, and needs no further confirmation.

The question, in reference to the Church so understood, is, Whether it can be truly affirmed that Christ is its Head? whether the admitted fact, that there are comprehended in this visible body more or fewer who have no vital connection with Christ, renders all statements regarding His Headship over it inappropriate? whether to a body so constituted He has any nearer relationship than He has, as being Head over all things? Should not all statements regarding His Headship be applied exclusively to the Church invisible, consisting only of those who are or shall be saved?

Doubtless there are, as I have already said,

some statements regarding the Church which cannot be applied with rigid exactness to the visible Church as a whole, or to any section of it. But by much the larger number of the references to the relation between Christ and His Church, contained in the Scriptures, are applicable without any strain upon their meaning to the visible Church; and some of these express a very close relationship. I have no hesitation, for example, in so applying the statements regarding Christ as the Head of the Church, although it is, confessedly, not composed exclusively of those who are vitally united to Him. The individual of whom it is true that Christ lives in him, dwelling in his heart by faith, is not therefore necessarily perfect. Paul, who asserted that Christ lived in him, was far from believing that he was perfect. He was conscious of much indwelling sin—of a law in his members warring against the law of his mind. But although not wholly sanctified in soul, and body, and spirit, he was yet vitally in union with Christ. The fact that there are diseased members in the body is not destructive of the body, nor fatal to its life. By slow degrees, it may be, the energy of the life expels the disease.

And in certain respects the same thing is true of the Church which is the body of Christ. The fact that there are members in it who are not partakers of spiritual life does not imply that Christ is not its Head. It may be, indeed, that the disease affecting some members may be so neglected, and may acquire such fatal ascendency in some particular branch of the Church, that it shall cease in any proper sense to be a church, and become a synagogue of Satan. It may die, or have only a carnal life. But, on the other hand, it may be so watchful, and so prompt in applying suitable remedies, and have in it such energy of life, that the disease in it may very little affect its healthful activities. In like manner, referring to the illustration which Christ Himself gives of the intimate relation between Himself and the Church, the vine has fruitless branches, which will be cut off and cast into the fire. But this fact does not affect the vital relation between the stem and the branches. They are all in the vine, and all its fruitfulness is due to the life which is in the stem, and which circulates through the plant; but some of the branches bear no fruit because of some defect or disease in them which hinders the free circulation of the sap of the stem.

Speaking of the Church, therefore, as a corporate body, we have abundant Scripture warrant for saying, that Christ is its Head, that He has the same close and vital relation to it as a body has to the head which directs it.

This is confirmed by the fact that the visible Church contains within it all the saints which are on the earth; and that it is through the organisation and ordinances of the Church that Christ usually gathers to Himself those whom He saves, and builds them up in their most holy faith. It pleases Him by the foolishness of preaching to save them that believe.

But enough has been said to vindicate the application to the visible Church of much, at least, of what Scripture says regarding the Headship of Christ over it, and accordingly I proceed to observe:—

First, That the Church owes its existence to Christ, and in this respect He is its Head. It is His creation. Apart from His redemption work, no such society could have existed. It consists of those who profess to be saved by His grace.

The Church is a community gathered out of the great human family—the chosen people of God, separated from the world, and placed in the nearest possible relation to Christ. It has been so since the first promise regarding the seed of the woman, under all various dispensations. It has made a covenant with God by sacrifice, and is a witness to the world of the grace that is in Jesus Christ. In the patriarchal ages it was so. Cain and Abel were representatives of the two classes—the one of the world and the other of Christ. When the wickedness of men became great on the earth, there was still left one preacher of righteousness, one elect family saved from the destroying flood. The Lord called Abraham from his own country, and separated him from his father's house, and made him His friend, and the father of all them that believe. His seed were the chosen people distinguished from all other nations. They were called the people of God, and were separated from the world by the faith which they professed, by the redemption they had experienced, and by various statutes and ordinances designed to preserve them as a peculiar people, and to testify to the grace which is in Christ. In the wilderness they are spoken of as the Church, and they were in covenant with God. To them "pertained the adoption, and the glory, and the covenants, and the giving of the law, and the service of God and the promises" (Romans ix. 4). And when the fulness of time had come, and the great propitiation so long prefigured and predicted had been made, the Church was greatly enlarged, and the Gentiles were made co-heirs of the promises with the seed of Abraham. But it was and is still the same Church, created and continued from generation to generation by the Word and Spirit of Christ—the same witness of the grace of God under the same covenant, and consisting of a people separated from the world, and held together by the profession of a common faith. It is true, indeed, that they are not all Israel who are of Israel, any more than it is true of any believer that he is perfectly sanctified. It may be that it shall become very faithless to its vocation, as the saints of God, personally, have fallen into great sins. Amputation is often necessary in a diseased body; and particular portions of the Church may become apostate, and cease to be of the Church catholic.

But the promise of God is not thereby made of none effect; and by adding to the Church of such as shall be saved, the Lord preserves His own creation, and by it testifies to the world of His redeeming grace.

Second, Christ as the Head of the Church provides it with all those means and instrumentalities whereby it is nourished and enabled to discharge the functions which belong to it, and which are necessary for preserving it in a healthy condition, and for increasing in strength. And He is personally present in these means, and gives them efficacy according to His pleasure.

First, and chiefly, He has given to the Church the revelation of His will contained in the Scriptures. This He did not do all at once, but by gradual development, as the Church was ripened in understanding, till the time when the whole mystery of godliness had been unfolded in fact, and the revelation of grace and truth was complete in Christ. The record of this revelation is the guide and supreme law of the Church. It is a lamp to her feet and a light to her path. It determines for her all spiritual truth, and prescribes all religious duty. It lays her under obligation to observe all things that are written in the law to do them. In regard to spiritual things, the Church acknowledges no authority but that of Christ speaking in His Word, and is subject to no law but His. On whatever matters He has made known His will, He is to be implicitly obeyed, notwithstanding what may be enjoined by any other authority; and that not merely because He is supreme Lord over all, but because of the relation between the Church and Himself. No relation can be closer than that which exists between the head and the body, and this is the relation between the Church and Christ. For although in many of her members this relation is not really vital, yet every member by profession and covenant stands in this relation. He professes to be redeemed by the blood of Christ, and to live by the faith of the Son of God—that his life is imparted by Christ, and sustained by Him. Christ is the Head of the body of which He is a member; but the seat of government and authority is in the Head, and without it the body has no capacity of action. All the members move in obedience to the Head. What it wills the body moves to carry into effect, and the members of the body are only subject to the Head, and do not act under the direction of another. My hands and feet obey me, and another has no control over them, except what is of constraint and force. Another man may lay hold on my hand, and lift it up, or he may bind the members of my body in chains, so that I cannot move, but he has no vital power over them. If I act in obedience to the command of another, it is because, first of all, he has subdued my will to his own. My members only move in obedience to the impulses of my own mind. If, therefore, in any real sense the Church is the body of Christ, it is subject exclusively to His sway, in the same manner as the members of my body are subject to my will. The Church, and all the living members of it, are obedient to the impulses of the will of Christ; and those of them who are not in living union with Christ are by profession bound to obey Him. There can be in the Church no divided authority, any more than there is in the human body. There cannot be two masters in the body of Christ.

It is important here also to remark, that the authority which Christ thus exercises is necessarily immediate. No power can interfere lawfully between the believer and Him, because the believer is a member of His body; and just because the Church is His body, all its members have the same relation to its Head. As the members of the body are not controlled by a power from without, so neither does one member regulate the action of another. All alike are connected with the Head, and all are subject to the purposes which the Head forms. My faith does not stand in the wisdom of man, but in the power of God; and herein consists at once the liberty of the Church and its obligation. It is entirely free from servitude to men; it is under obligation in all respects to obey the will of Christ. In so far as I am faithful to Christ, it must be His will that moves and constrains me.

Such a doctrine as this does not, as we shall see, supersede the use and necessity of pastors and teachers in the Church, whom the members of it are enjoined to obey in the Lord. These are organs and instruments through whom Christ expresses His will to me, but I must for myself ascertain whether it is the will of Christ which they express. "To the law and to the testimony, if they speak not according to this word, it is because there is no light in them." I owe no subjection to them; I am subject only to Christ. To be obedient to them is not to serve Christ. It is only when they hold forth to me the will of Christ, and when I recognise it as His, that, in submitting myself to them, I am obeying Christ. And this fact lays upon each member of the Church the responsibility of ascertaining for himself. and from the written revealed Word, what Christ would have him to do. As He has been pleased to record His will, I am bound to search the Scriptures to ascertain what He would have me to believe and do. In the Church there is no esoteric doctrine for a particular class. What Christ has recorded for one He has recorded for all. Ministers are ambassadors whose credentials are open to all the world, and these define the limits of their commission. The words they speak must be Christ's recorded words, if they are to have any authority. There is thus in the Church a more perfect liberty than is enjoyed in any kingdom of this world. A written and fixed law is necessary in any community, in order to the enjoyment of liberty. At first, indeed, laws seem to be a restriction on liberty, rather than a security for freedom. But it is not really so. In any nation freedom must have, as its security and basis, a published code of laws. Otherwise people are at the mercy of any one who has the inclination and the power to injure them; otherwise you have no defence against the exercise of caprice, or the invasion of brute force. All sorts of tyranny and oppression are possible and likely when you are at the mercy of a powerful man's will. But with a published law you know what to do and to expect, and you can regulate your conduct by its requirements. The law, indeed, may be very unjust and oppressive, but under its shelter you have some province which cannot be invaded, and within that province the law is your shield and protector. Without it you are exposed to interminable and unexpected invasion from every side. But even in the freest earthly nation liberty is not perfect. The published law requires judges to interpret and administer it, and their interpretation may be wrong,—the result not of a clear intelligence, but of prejudice and passion. Doubtless it is often so in times of excitement in a community, but you have no remedy against the judge's decision. However erroneous it may be, you must submit to it, and incur the loss which the error implies. But it is not so in the Church, which is the Kingdom of Christ. In it there is no judge whose exclusive prerogative it is to interpret the law. Every member of it is under obligation to examine for himself the Statute Book of Heaven, and to form his own judgment as to what it enjoins or forbids. In this kingdom you judge the officers by the law; they are always on their trial before the Church. You are required to test by the law the verity of their verdict and statement. Their judgments have no binding obligation, but the law has.

But besides, and above all this, Christ gives Himself to the Church along with His Word. By His Spirit He is always present in it, giving light by which to read the Word, and rendering it effectual for the purposes for which it has been written. Apart from this the Scriptures would avail nothing as regards the salvation of man. For "the natural man receiveth not the things of the Spirit of God; for they are foolishness unto Him: neither can He know them, because they are spiritually discerned" (1 Cor. ii. 14).

Therefore Christ, before entering within the veil as the great High Priest over the household of faith, gave this faithful promise to His people, "The Comforter, which is the Holy Ghost, whom the Father will send in My name, He shall teach you all things, and bring all things to your remembrance whatsoever I have said unto you" (John xiv. 26). "When He, the Spirit of Truth, is come, He will guide you into all truth" (John xvi. 13). And this Spirit abides in the Church always, the witness of the exaltation of Christ, and the imparter to men of the fruits of His redemption. Such a guide and interpreter of truth every member of the Church may have, if he earnestly seek Him, for Christ has said, "If ye being evil know how to give good gifts unto your children; how much more shall your Heavenly Father give the Holy Spirit to them that ask Him" (Luke xi. 13). He is the one safe and infallible teacher of both pastors and people. By Him Christ is always present with them, and living in them, "the Spirit of wisdom and understanding in the fear of the Lord:" so bountiful is the provision which Christ has maed for the Church, and so close is the relation He sustains to it as its living Head. Yet it is true that there are always in the Church those who have not the Spirit of Truth. They do not desire His teaching, for they do not love the truth, and choose rather to walk in darkness ; and it is true even of those who have the Spirit, that they do not always in singleness of heart yield themselves to His guidance. Just as no man in this life is perfectly sanctified, so no man and no church is infallible. The holiest men, the purest churches, are prone to yield to the worldly influences which encompass them, and to be beguiled from the simplicity of the truth. It is the pure in heart who see God. It is those who are wholly transformed into the likeness of Christ, who see Him as He is. And because no church is free from sin, no church is free from error. Yet it is true that the Church is the pillar and ground of the truth, shining indeed often very obscurely amid thick mists of prejudice and passion, and, more than all, of pride and self-sufficiency. "The meek will He guide in judgment ; and the meek will He teach His way." "The secret of the Lord is with them that fear Him ; and He will show them His covenant" (Psalm xxv. 9, 14). It is those who do the will of God that know His doctrine.

Christianity is essentially social. Believers have in Christ a common bond of union. They are members of one body; and they are members of one another. Hence it is that there is a Church, the members of which are united together by the bonds of a common faith. But it is essential to the harmonious action of a community that there shall be officers of administration; and Christ has provided these for the Church. When He ascended on high, after having finished His work on the earth, "He gave some, apostles; and some, prophets; and some, evangelists; and some, pastors and teachers; for the perfecting of the saints, for the work of the ministry, for the edifying of the body of Christ" (Eph. iv. 11, 12). He has defined the functions they are to discharge, and their relation both to Himself and to the body of which He is the Head. They are at once the servants of the Church and its rulers. They are to be highly esteemed in love for their work's sake, and obedience to them as rulers is enjoined. But they are not lords over God's heritage, but helpers of His people's faith. Their function is in the Church visible as incorporated, and organised into a community professing the faith of Christ; and it is purely administrative. They are not legislators, but administer the laws of Christ. They do not stand between the members of the Church and Christ. Their highest function is to show to men the things of Christ, and in Christ's stead to beseech men to be reconciled to God; and within the Church to take care that the laws of Christ are duly observed. They are gifts of Christ to the Church, and are under obligation to act for Him and in His name. He holds them in His hand. They have no standing but in Him, and no authority except the declarations of His Word. It is by this Word they bear rule. Apart from this, their words, whether as commands, or promises, or reproofs, or instruction, are of no weight or authority.

The fact that these officers are gifts of Christ implies also plainly enough, that they must be of such a kind as Christ has authorised and ordained to be ministers in the Church. They are sent by Him, and they are endowed with needed gifts by Him. Their place and office are designated and limited by Him. But it is a question of special importance to the Church, how its members are to ascertain that Christ has appointed them, and that their position is not usurped. Christ, although present in the Church, is invisible, and speaks to the Church only by His written Word. His officers do not bring from Him a special mandate. He does not say, Here is the man to whom I have given my commission for executing My will. Under the former dispensation office in the Church was hereditary; and when the Christian Church was first organised, its officers gave unmistakable manifestations that Christ had sent them. They were endowed with miraculous gifts, and by the exercise of these proved that they were sent by Him. They cast out devils, and in His name did many wonderful works, and the Holy Spirit set His seal upon their work. "Am I not an apostle?" Paul said: "Am I not free? have I not seen Christ? are not ye my work in the Lord?" (1 Cor. ix. 1.) But, in process of time, those who were to bear rule in the Church, possessed no such endowments; and the Church had to be guided by other considerations in recognising and submitting to those officers authorised by Christ. But He did not leave the Church without sufficient directions to guide its members in the matter of teaching and government, if with singleness of eye and heart they were prepared to act upon His counsel.

And one of the first things they would have to consider was, of what sort their guides and rulers were to be. In the passage in Ephesians already quoted, there are four classes of officers mentioned. These are apostles, prophets, evangelists, and pastors and teachers. The apostles were those who had seen the Lord in the body, and had been directly of His appointment, and therefore necessarily were only temporary officers without successors. Prophets were a gift to the infant Church, and the gift has not, in fact, been perpetuated. There remain therefore only two of the four classes—namely, evangelists, and pastors, and teachers; but to these must be added also deacons, as mentioned in the Acts, and in the pastoral epistles, in which pastors and teachers are spoken of under the name of elders, and sometimes overseers. This then is the permanent provision which Christ has made for the guidance and government of the Church—evangelists, who have their representatives in our modern missionaries, who have not the charge of any particular flock, but are employed in planting and organising new churches from among the heathen; and besides these, elders or overseers, consisting of those who are rulers, and those who, besides ruling, labour in word and doctrine; and deacons who do the work of rule and service in particular congregations. There are no other officers than these, who can be regarded as of Christ's providing, and they are sufficient for all purposes of administration.

But no man is entitled to assume any of these offices for himself, and the question accordingly is raised, in what way they are to be called and appointed. In their appointment it is clear enough that no one outside the Church has any thing to do; and as within the Church no one member has superiority over another, but all are brethren, necessarily the choice of those who are to bear rule over them must belong to all the members; for it is no part of the function of office-bearers to elect. Office-bearers have, indeed, an important function in reference to those who are called to office. It belongs to them to judge of their qualifications, and formally to ordain and admit to office those who are elected.

But how are the members of the Church, or of a particular congregation, to determine their choice, in conformity with the will of Christ? In the choice of pastors they are greatly aided by the arrangement which common-sense, and the example of Christ in the training of the apostles, warrant; and accordingly provision is made by the Church for the special training for this office of those who seem to be endowed with special gifts for it. And besides this, and in regard to other officers, they must be guided by the fact, that certain parties seem to possess the character and qualifications necessary for the proper discharge of the duties of the office. It is the recognition by the Church of such qualifications that is the ground or warrant of the call. The pastor of a Church is not lawfully such, without this call and election. He is not the born ruler of the Church, but is born of the Church. The Church was not made for him, but he for it. The Church first exists, and then pastors spring up in it for its edification.

The functions of these office-bearers are prescribed by Christ, and are limited by Him. To evangelists it belongs to plant and organise churches gathered from among the heathen, or the world of unbelievers. To deacons belongs the ministry to the poor, and in general the collection and distribution of what the Church contributes for the maintenance and diffusion of the Gospel. The eldership have a different and a wider function. They are both teachers and rulers in the Church. They are rulers simply as ministers of Christ, and their power is ministerial or administrative. Their function as Church rulers has been defined with sufficient clearness, by calling it the power of the keys. It is by this name expressly that Christ has committed to them their power as rulers. It is the power of opening and of shutting—the power of admitting to membership or office in the Church, and the power of expulsion or exclusion. This is clearly expressed in various Scripture statements: "We beseech you, brethren," says Paul, "to know them which labour among you, and are over you in the Lord, and admonish you; and to esteem them very highly in love for their work's sake"

(1 Thess. v. 12, 13)—a statement which implies that there are rulers, or oversmen in the Church, —over them in the Lord, not exercising an independent authority, but as ministers of Christ. Again, in another place, he says, "Remember them which have the rule over you, who have spoken unto you the word of God" (Heb. xiii. 7); an admonition from which it appears that the function of Church rulers is inseparably bound up with that of teaching, publicly or privately, the Word of God. Again, as indicating what is implied in their ruling, he says, "A man that is an heretic, after the first and second admonition, reject" (Titus iii. 10),—an injunction implying the capacity and power of determining what heresy is, and of excommunicating him who is found guilty of it. This power of administration is still further illustrated by the fact that in the controversy which arose in the Apostolic Churches regarding circumcision, it was the apostles and elders who assembled together to consider the question, and their determination was authoritative in the Church; for we read afterwards that, as they went through the cities, they delivered them the decrees to keep; which were or-

dained of the apostles and elders that were at Jerusalem.

To these officers, and to them exclusively, belongs all administrative power in the Church, and the framing of such regulations as may be necessary for the orderly and decent conducting of its affairs. They alone are required to be duly qualified for this rule. They are held responsible for its proper exercise, and the promises of help and reward, in exercising it faithfully, are addressed solely to them. Their qualifications are detailed at length in 1 Timothy iii., and these are required of no other class of men. Their responsibility in discharging the duties of their office is thus described: "Feed the flock of God which is among you, taking the oversight thereof, not by constraint, but willingly; not for filthy lucre, but of a ready mind; neither as being lords over God's heritage, but being ensamples to the flock. And when the Chief Shepherd shall appear, ye shall receive a crown of glory that fadeth not away" (1 Peter v. 2-4). And the promise to them of all sufficient help is conveyed in the assurance: "Lo, I am with you alway, even unto the end of the world" (Matt. xxviii. 20). To them alone moreover, is the obedience declared to be due, which is incumbent on church members in Church affairs, "Obey them that have the rule over you, and submit yourselves; for they watch for your souls, as they that must give account" (Heb. xiii. 17). The intervention, therefore, in these matters, of any other authority, is at once a usurpation of the prerogative of Christ, and an invasion of the liberties of the Church, which cannot fail to be injurious to its spiritual life, by separating it more or less from its conscious dependence on its Great Head, and thus involving the loss of that strength and vitality which result from abiding in Him.

LECTURE III.

RELATIONS OF CHURCH AND STATE.

It is impossible that the Church and the State should stand entirely apart from each other. Wherever a church exists, there exists within the same territory two kingdoms—a kingdom of nature and a kingdom of grace; and their mutual relations have been in all ages a fruitful cause of controversy and strife. It is by no means easy to draw a sharp line of distinction between the secular and the sacred, and the tendency of the one to encroach upon the province of the other has constantly manifested itself. On the one hand, the State has often failed to recognise within its borders a kingdom distinct from itself, and has usurped the control over all things, sacred as well as civil; and, on the other hand, if the Church has acknowledged a secular kingdom separate from itself, it has often regarded this kingdom as subordinate to itself, and has practically engrossed the whole power of the State, making the State obedient to its behests. But such usurpation, whether on the part of the State or of the Church, has always proved deeply injurious to both. The State does not strengthen itself, but becomes feeble and degraded when it enslaves the Church; and the Church is secularised in its whole character when it usurps power over the State, and its management of State affairs has proved itself to be the most corrupt and tyrannical.

The two kingdoms cannot be identified or amalgamated; they are different in their origin and in their aims. The kingdom of God is primarily and essentially in the hearts of men whose affections are swayed by Him, and whose minds apprehend His will, and are loyally obedient to it. It is a kingdom within men—a spiritual kingdom, in which the Lord reigns, and in the souls of whose subjects He works both to *will* and to *do* of His good pleasure. It is a kingdom that exists wherever there is a heart loyal to the Divine authority, and responsive to the claims of Divine love. It finds a place among all races of men, and in all classes and conditions of society; it enthrones itself in the heart of monarchs, and manifests its power over the meanest slave. It is not conterminous with any of the kingdoms of this world; and, when organised into a commonwealth, its laws are different from theirs. Its power is not that of the sword, and its authority is not that of constraint. Its weapons are not carnal, and its conquests are not stained with blood. It is sustained and extended solely by the power of persuasion. It has its own peculiar field of legislation, and its own modes of service. It does not necessarily enter into conflict with temporal kingdoms, because it is of a different order from these, and its operations lie within a different sphere. The rendering to Cæsar the things that are Cæsar's does not hinder the rendering to God the things that are God's. The two kingdoms are not on the same plane. The one is outward, and the other is chiefly internal. The one dominates in the things that are temporal, the sphere of the other lies in the things which are spiritual and eternal. The kingdom of God does not come with observation—with the blare of trumpets, and the tumult of war, and the shout of victory. It comes as the springtime comes to the earth, at whose gentle breathing the buds begin to shoot forth, and the singing of birds is heard, and a new life is manifested in all the domain of Nature. It comes speaking of peace on earth, and goodwill to men. It comes as the bearer of gracious truth, beseeching men to be reconciled to God; and there are hearts and minds opened to apprehend and receive the truth, which enters like the seed-corn into the soil, and transforms what before was merely earth into a fruit-bearing plant, living and beautiful, and bearing the impress of its heavenly origin. And those who so receive the truth are drawn together, and form a society, not regulated by human device, but which is organised and directed by the power which has called it into being. It does not frame its own constitution, and is not subject to laws of its own devising. It is a Divine creation, and its members owe allegiance to the Lord who has redeemed it, and gathered it from among the mass of the people. By profession, at least, if not in mind and heart, its members are bound to this allegiance, and live by the faith of the Son of God, who loved them and gave Himself for them. They are a peculiar people, a kingdom of priests. They are not of the world, and the kingdom of which they are members is not of the world. They are gathered out of it, and separated from it. The Church is not a province or colony of any of the world's empires: it is distinct from them all, and independent of them all.

Even when the predicted time comes, when the kingdoms of this world shall become the kingdoms of our God and of His Christ, the Church and State will not be amalgamated. They will still have distinct institutions and modes of administration. There will still be Church rulers, and State judges and magistrates taking cognisance of different matters, although it may be in reference to the same individual. In such a condition of things the civil magistrate will rule in the fear of God, and his subjects will yield obedience to him, not for wrath, but for conscience' sake; but the Church ruler will also have his distinct province of administration, and continue to exercise the power of the keys. In such a state of society every citizen of the commonwealth will probably be also a member of the Church, but his responsibilities and duties, as citizen and church member, will be different; and there may be offences against the Church of which the State ruler can, and ought to, take no cognizance. Even as in the present condition of things, there are many citizens who are also church members, but their relation to the Church is not the same as their relation to the State. The State ruler takes cognizance of crimes, and the Church ruler takes cognizance of sins. This distinction has often been practically disregarded, but always with such injurious effects as to show that by so doing they are traversing the order which God has ordained.

Even under the Old Testament dispensation the distinction between Church and State existed. Before the seed of Abraham became a nation, they lived as a peculiar people, chosen of God to preserve in the world the knowledge of Him who had redeemed them. When they migrated into Egypt they were not amalgamated with its people. They lived apart and alone. They did not even eat with the Egyptians. They had their own religious observances and sacrifices. When they were reduced to servitude, and had hard taskmasters set over them, and were made the victims of cruel laws, they did not become Egyptians. They still retained the knowledge of and worshipped the one living and true God. Even Moses, who was the adopted son of Pharaoh's daughter, and was educated at the king's court, did not become an Egyptian. We may rest assured it was not by the learning of Egypt that he knew the true God, nor was it by the observance of its laws that he vindicated his oppressed brethren. And when, by the mighty hand of God, he led them forth from their bondage, and became their lawgiver, and organised them into a nation, they still remained a peculiar people. Their laws, among other objects, were expressly framed to keep them wholly separate from other nations—conservators of the truth of God. God was their Judge, and Lawgiver, and King. But even then, although every member of the community was also a member of the Church, there were still distinct provinces of administration in the Church and in the State. Their priests were not kings, nor were their kings priests. The function of the civil ruler, whether judge or king, was distinct from that of the priest. To the priest belonged the service of the altar; to the civil ruler, the administration of justice between man and man. Nor was any intrusion of the one into the proper province of the other treated with impunity. Even in the wilderness, in the case of Korah and his company, God, by terrible things in righteousness, vindicated the sacredness of the service of the Tabernacle; and in the time of the Kings, on the occasion of bringing the Ark of the Covenant to Jerusalem, in the days of David; as also in the case of King Uzziah, God showed how jealously He guarded the domain of the priests. Israel was indeed a holy nation, but within it was a peculiar class set apart for sacred service. All the other nations of the world had their *golden age* in the past, revealing, by their conception of things, their consciousness of degenerating influences drifting them into ever-deepening degradation. Israel alone had its *golden age* in the future, and was saved by hope; and all the institutions and rites which were designed to cherish that hope formed a peculiar department of service, into which none might intrude save those who were ordained for it of God.

And when Christ came, and the wall of partition was broken down, when the Gentiles became fellow-heirs with the Jews of the Divine promises, the distinction between the civil and the sacred was not obliterated. There was no longer indeed a priestly caste and an altar, and bloody sacrifices. Christ is the one Priest, and the one sacrifice and altar, of the New Testament Church; and He has entered within the veil, there to appear in the presence of God for us. Every believer has access to God through Him, and is in Him a consecrated priest having entrance into the holiest by His blood. But all the more, therefore, is the distinction between the civil and the sacred preserved—all the more conspicuous it is that there is a kingdom of God separate from the kingdoms of this world. On the very day when Christ was crucified this distinction was declared by Him, and seems to have been dimly apprehended even by Pontius Pilate. "As a sheep before its shearers is dumb, so He opened not His mouth." He made no complaint against the cruel injustice He suffered. But Pilate gave Him the opportunity of announcing a truth which might be of eminent service both to statesmen and church officers in all the future ages, and His mouth was opened to speak it. Pilate, astonished at His silence, said, "Speakest Thou not unto me? knowest Thou not that I have power to crucify Thee, and have power to release Thee? Jesus answered, Thou couldest have no power at all against Me, except it were given thee from above; therefore he that delivered Me unto thee hath the greater sin" (John xix. 10, 11.) The power thou hast, the power of life and death, is not thine inherently. It is not a power given thee even by Cæsar. It is from above—a power given thee of God, that thou mightest be a terror to evil-doers, and a praise and protection to them who do well; and to God thou art responsible for the use of it. He who delivered Me unto thee was well aware of this, and the greater sin is his, in seeking to pervert this ordinance of God into an instrument of injustice and wrong. The God who gave thee power is a righteous God, and if thou usest it in unrighteousness thou must answer it to Him.

This has a direct and very important bearing upon what occurred in a previous interview with Pilate. The accusation against Christ was, that

He was acknowledged as a King, and Pilate said to Him, "Art Thou the King of the Jews? Jesus answered, My kingdom is not of this world; if My kingdom were of this world, then would My servants fight, that I should not be delivered to the Jews; but now is My kingdom not from hence. Pilate therefore said unto Him, Art Thou a King then? Jesus answered, Thou sayest that I am a King. To this end was I born, and for this cause came I into the world, that I should bear witness unto the truth. Every one that is of the truth heareth My voice" (John xviii. 36, 37). Here then are two kings and two kingdoms, the one within the other, and yet forming no part of it. The king of the one is Cæsar, or his subordinate, Pilate; the King of the other is Jesus. The one kingdom is of this world, and the other is not of this world; and therefore they do not necessarily come into collision with each other. They are in different spheres, although both of them are on the earth, and the subjects of both may be the same. The king of the one has the power of the sword. This Pilate asserted, and Jesus confirmed. Pilate had power to kill or to preserve alive under responsibility to God who gave him this power, and Jesus acknowledged that he had it. But his power was not a power over all things, although it was over all persons. For there was another kingdom, having no power over temporal things, and exercising no compulsion. It was a kingdom consisting of those who apprehended the truth, and became obedient to its dictates—who of their own free will subjected themselves to the authority of the heavenly King. The Jews thought they were sure of obtaining the condemnation of Jesus because he was a King—sure that Pilate would suffer no one to live who asserted royal authority which was not derived from the Roman Emperor. But Pilate saw no incompatibility between the two kingdoms. He was not offended because Jesus declared himself to be a King. The Roman Empire was not endangered, nor the power of Cæsar abridged by the existence of the kingdom of Christ. In hearing and obeying the truth there was nothing to impair the allegiance which was due to the empire. On the contrary, there was much to establish it upon a sure foundation, to make the loyalty of the people rest not on the fear of vengeance, but on the authority of conscience and the fear of God. For the truth they learned taught them that the powers that be are ordained of God; and that in resisting them they would be resisting the ordinance of God. Therefore they, of all the subjects of the empire, would "render to all their dues: tribute to whom tribute is due; custom to whom custom; fear to whom fear; honour to whom honour." And yet this did not hinder them being the loyal subjects of another King, to whom they owed allegiance of another kind. True allegiance to Cæsar, indeed, rested on their allegiance to Christ. Loyalty to Him would constrain them to "render to Cæsar the things that are Cæsar's," but it would constrain them also to withhold obedience to him in the things of God. For Christ has a kingdom in which He is the only Lord, and in which His authority is exclusively to be acknowledged. He is supreme, the Lord of all lords, who both determines the limits of His own authority and those of Cæsar. But their domains are distinct, and their powers are not necessarily conflicting. Pilate recognised the fact that the kingdom of Christ, as he defined it, was in a region beyond his control. Truth, and adherence to truth, were out of the sphere of the imperial government.

It did not follow, indeed, that the powers could not come into conflict. There might be invasion and usurpation by the one power or the other. The two powers were not conflicting only when each of them confined itself within its own province. Cæsar might attempt to determine what the truth was which men were bound to believe and obey; and, on the other hand, church rulers might arrogate the power of regulating State affairs. The safety and welfare of each lay in recognising and acting upon the fact, that wherever a church existed there were two kingdoms, distinct from and independent of each other, each having its own sphere of action and authority. There might be difficulty, indeed, in defining in every case the limits of their respective provinces—a difficulty which it would be easy enough to remove, if the rulers in each were of single eye and of pure heart. But human nature being as it is, it was in the highest degree probable that the line of demarcation would be traversed from both sides to the mutual injury of Church and State. This evil, in fact, had already begun when Christ was defining to Pilate the nature of His kingdom, and He was Himself the first victim of the transgression.

It was not the Romans who made the first aggression upon the liberties of the Church. In the progress of their conquests, they did not impose their religion upon the people they subdued. They did not interfere with the worship and religious observances of the subject nations. Thus the Jews retained, under the sway of Rome, their temple, and sacrifices, and priesthood. The Romans respected, as in other cases, their religion, and protected them in the exercise of its rites. It was their civil and political government only that perished. But the priesthood, left in the exercise of the sole power remaining, invaded the domain of the civil ruler. They were not content with excommunicating Jesus and His disciples. They assumed also the power of the sword, and, unable themselves to put Jesus to death, they invoked the aid of the Roman ruler to accomplish their purpose. They acted, indeed, the very part which the Popish Church in after ages so cruelly practised. But except in the case of Jesus, who confessedly was unjustly sacrificed to the malice of the Jews, the Roman rulers defended Christians from their fury.

But this state of things did not long continue. The Jews having rejected and crucified Christ, whose kingdom was so different from their ideal kingdom of the expected Messiah, became impatient of the Roman yoke, and in Palestine, and in all places of their dispersion, conspired to cast it off. Their sedition excited the wrath of the imperial power, and roused against them a hostility which terminated in the destruction of Jerusalem, and in their extinction as a nation. Perhaps the earliest persecution of Christians by the Romans was due to the fact of their being regarded as Jews, of whom indeed a large portion of the Christian Church primarily consisted; and the churches which sprung up in many cities of the empire, and in Rome itself, had their beginning in the Jewish synagogues.

But very soon, on other grounds, Rome became intolerant, and endeavoured to exterminate the Church. Soon after its government had assumed the imperial form, its emperors became the representatives of the gods, and homage to the emperor was homage rendered to Jupiter, and the refusal of this homage was a rebellion against the State. But Christians could not pay this homage without renouncing their faith, and therefore were dealt with as rebels, and persecuted with more or less severity, even by emperors who were otherwise just and wise, because they believed that the preservation of the empire was involved in the maintenance of that worship which Christians could not observe. Thus, in their turn, the Roman rulers invaded the domain of the Church and the rights of conscience, and involved themselves in the sin so often repeated in after ages. They enforced laws which it was beyond their province to make, and became persecutors, just as in our own land Christians were put to death under the Stuarts, ostensibly not because they were Christians, but men in rebellion against the law of the land ; and in more recent times they were covered with all manner of obloquy for refusing obedience to a law which was an invasion of the rights of conscience and the liberty of the Church.

Notwithstanding the persecution to which it was subjected, however, the Church grew and multiplied until it became a power which a wise ruler was bound to recognise ; and, amid the confusion which prevailed, its aid was sought by Constantine to place him on the imperial throne. Meanwhile, however, the Church had undergone a great change, and had departed very far from the simplicity of its original constitution. Instead of the elders and deacons, which had been originally its sole office-bearers, it had rank above rank of ecclesiastical officials, separating the higher order of them, at least, more and more from the body of the members. As the Church increased in numbers, it afforded scope for the exercise of worldly ambition; and already, before it had received the patronage of Constantine, there were in it all the elements of what grew, in course of time, into the enormous and tyrannical power of the Papacy. Already there was a clerical priesthood, and the beginning of a lordship over God's heritage, and the assumption of temporal power. The false and fatal assumption that the Church, which was to embrace all the people of the world, must be one visible corporation, lay at the root of most of those inventions which corrupted it, and inevitably led to the conclusion that it must have one supreme ruler or pope. The patronage of Constantine in some respects rather checked than fostered this growing evil. In relation to Christianity he assumed very much the place which the heathen emperors had occupied in relation to paganism. Their war banners represented the gods whom they worshipped, and the emperor as their vicegerent; and the cross was the emblem pictured on his banner. He assumed to be very much the vicegerent of the Prince of the kings of the earth. He conferred upon the Church indeed large endowments, and fortified it with many immunities, but at the same time he subjected it to his supreme authority, both in doctrine and in discipline. He called councils indeed, but their decrees were largely of his determination. In fact, in obedience to his caprice, the two first councils pronounced contradictory decrees. Having removed the seat of empire to Byzantium, the Western Church was more remote from his influence and less affected by it; and, in the course of the succeeding centuries, the Eastern Church continued subject to the temporal power, as it is at this day, while the Western Church assumed dominion over it.

In his "Civitas Dei," Augustine has very

clearly expressed the views entertained, and eventually carried into effect by the Western Church. The principles of the Eastern Church were not different, indeed, only they were never embodied in action, for we have this saying of Chrysostom, "The emperor governs the body, the priest governs the mind; therefore the emperor must bow his head under the hand of the priest." A heathen State, according to Augustine, is a *Civitas Diaboli.* Singly and unassisted a State cannot fulfil its purposes: it requires justice, and justice can only exist with the true worship of God. It must use its influence of power in the service of the true God, who reveals Himself in the Church. It receives its true mission and consecration in yielding allegiance to the true Church. It receives the obedience of the Church in all temporal matters; but when it does not obey the Church in spiritual things it works its own destruction; and the Church alone can decide what are spiritual matters. Heresy is a crime, the suppression of which is incumbent on the State. The unity of the Church must be preserved by all means at her disposal; and the State, as her commissioned agent, must by force, if necessary, aid her in preserving it. The individual stands to the Church in the relation of a minor. He is to believe on her authority, and cannot be saved without her. It is of primary concern that he should belong to her communion, and it is better that he should belong to it by compulsion than not at all. The Church, from being herself persecuted, thus became a persecuting Church. It is lamentable to find such principles advocated by such a man as Augustine, who had such clear perceptions of the doctrines of grace which became a precious legacy to the Church. But the legacy of his Church principles also produced fruit even more abundantly of a pernicious kind, which ripened into the most daring assumptions of the Papal tyranny. These assumptions were not indeed always and in every place submitted to. The Lord always preserved a seed to serve Him. But it would be beside my purpose to note the incidents during the middle ages of resistance to Papal usurpation in Britain and elsewhere.

I proceed at once, therefore, to a review of the relations between Church and State as exhibited at the Reformation, especially by Luther and

Calvin. It is to be regretted, in the case of Luther, that, great as his endowments were, and however precious the fruit of his labours, his mind was either too exclusively engrossed with preaching orally or through the press the saving doctrines of the Gospel; or else he was peculiarly deficient in the faculty and power of organisation, and paid but little regard to the government and discipline of the Church. So heedless was he of this, indeed, that he would have been well content to leave untouched the Church organisation as it stood, if he had found it possible to harmonise it with the vital doctrines of the Gospel. He broke with the Papacy only when he found its pretensions to be in flat contradiction to his great doctrine of justification by faith. It might have been expected, therefore, and it was what actually took place, that in reforming the Church he would only remove those forms and institutions which he found directly obstructing his great aim.

But it was impossible for him to remain in the Romish Church. Its principles were in conflict with his inmost experience as a believer. It assumed the power of saving sinners; and he found, after earnest trial, that it could not save him. Its doctrine was, that the visible community of all the faithful constituting the Church had perpetuated in it the power of taking away sin, and sanctifying men, which Christ by His Spirit exercised by means of an apostleship instituted by Him, and continued in all after ages. To the bishops, who were the direct successors of the apostles, were transmitted by ordination the same spiritual gifts bestowed by Christ on their predecessors; and they, in like manner, transmitted them to the priests. The episcopate, therefore, was the organ and exclusive vehicle of the Holy Spirit, and was to mankind the fountain of all grace. But Luther had learned, both by bitter and sweet experience, that God's way of saving sinners was far different from this. Without the mediation of any priest or bishop, he was justified freely by the grace of God, through faith in Jesus Christ; and it was even so that every sinner must be saved. If personal faith, therefore, alone determines a man's participation in redemption, he does not need the mediation of a consecrated priest. He is himself a priest, having access to God by the one Mediator. "Man's invention," he said, "has discovered that the Pope, the bishops, the priests, and the monks, are called the spiritual or ecclesiastical states; and that the princes, nobles, citizens, and peasants are called the secular state or laity. A fine story, forsooth! But let no man be terrified by such fictions. All Christians belong to the spiritual state; nor is there any other difference between them than that of the functions they discharge. We have all one baptism, one faith, and it is this alone which makes the spiritual man, or the Christian nature. If there were not a higher consecration within us than that conferred by pope or bishop, no mere consecration of pope or bishop could ever make a priest. The consecration by the bishop is therefore nothing more than this: that in place of, and personating the whole congregation, each one of whom possesses equal powers, he selects one particular member, and directs him to exercise this power on behalf of the rest. A priest, therefore, is nothing else than an office-holder. The clergy, as they call them, have in reality nothing to distinguish them but their functions. They all belong to the same estate, but all have not the same work to perform, and to that extent all of them are not equal." "The Church, however," he further says, "is not merely a community, like other societies, of outward observances and usages: it is the community, above all, of faith, and of the Holy Spirit indwelling in the hearts of its members."

He distinguishes between the visible and the invisible Church—the latter consisting of those who are really reconciled to God; the former containing also those who, though unreconciled, profess to be. A church proves itself to be a Church of Christ by the preaching of the Gospel, and by the administration of the Sacraments in conformity with the Gospel. "For real unity of the Church," according to the Augsburg Confession, "it is sufficient to agree on the teaching of the Gospel and the administration of the Sacraments; nor is it necessary that there should be everywhere the same traditions, usages, and ceremonies, all of which are instituted by man." "The Gospel," Luther declares, "brings no new laws on the relations of civil society, but commands all men to obey the existing laws, whether made by heathens or any others, just as we must all submit to the seasons and their changes." And the

Augsburg Confession says, "The ecclesiastical and civil powers are not to be confounded. The ecclesiastical power has its own command to preach the Gospel and administer the Sacraments. Let it not intrude upon another's office; let it not transfer the kingdoms of the world; let it not abrogate the laws of magistrates, nor withdraw from their lawful obedience, nor hinder the execution of judgments touching any civil ordinances or contracts; let it not prescribe laws to governors concerning the form of the commonwealth, — since Christ sayeth, 'My kingdom is not of this world.'" But while the independence of the State is thus vindicated, Luther also excluded State interference in ecclesiastical matters. "God," he says, "cannot, and will not, allow any one but Himself alone to rule the soul. As to faith, that is a free work,—no one can be forced to it. Whenever, therefore, the temporal power presumes to legislate for the soul, it encroaches upon the government of God, and seduces and corrupts the soul. God alone can know the hearts of men: it is impossible and futile, therefore, to command or constrain by violence any man to believe this way or that. Let them command as strictly and rage as furiously as they will, they cannot force the people, further than to follow them with their mouths and hands." "Heresy," he also said, "is something spiritual that cannot be cut out with steel, nor burned with fire, nor drowned with water."

Thus far Luther's conceptions of the relation between Church and State are clear and decisive, and abundantly satisfactory. But they were incomplete: there is in them no provision for the government of the Church. It was a great thing for him to say, "I have wielded only the weapon of His Word, and have struck straight at the heart; I have left God to dispose and govern, and the Word to operate;" but the Church, as a visible community, needed officers of administration: it required discipline as well as worship. Ministers, he taught, should be chosen by the community, but their function was merely teaching the Gospel and administering the Sacraments. Later on, however, both he and Melancthon held that magistrates should forbid heresies and punish heretics; and, amid the political revolutions consequent upon the Reformation, which it is not our business to trace, this was the issue, so far as concerned the government of the Church: that the Church became wholly enslaved to the State, having no independent jurisdiction of its own. The civil and ecclesiastical powers were merged in the territorial princes, who governed the Church by the establishment of consistories, composed partly of jurists and partly of theologians; and the Church and State came to be identified,—the citizens of the commonwealth being all church members, and the government of the church being merely a department of State administration. Such an arrangement infinitely weakened the power of the Reformation and arrested its progress. It ceased to be a great vital force, overcoming all obstacles by its Divine energy.

Calvin had no part in the earlier movements of the Reformation in Switzerland, and when he came upon the scene he had many things to undo; and this he was able only to accomplish imperfectly. Zwingle had already done what the German princes were led to do. He entirely rejected all ecclesiastical authority, and merged into one the Church and the State. According to his conception every government ought to be Christian, and to administer its affairs in conformity with the Word of God; and the same government sufficed for both Church and State, having different departments—the spiritual and the secular. There was consequently no struggle, as in other lands, for the independence of the Church. Zwingle, the preacher, had no hesitation in taking his place in the council of the Canton of Zurich, and the whole organisation of the Church was determined by it. At Berne and at Basle the same method was substantially adopted. At Geneva, Calvin did what he could to rectify this state of things, and to establish for the Church a distinct and independent jurisdiction. Confessedly he was only partially successful, for in 1542 he wrote, "We have now an ecclesiastical tribunal and such a form of religious discipline as these troublous times will allow." He was not able to realise his ideal, but he made Geneva the centre and starting point of a far-reaching movement, which gave its form to many of the churches of the Reformation. In his view it was a fundamental principle that the Church and State were distinct and independent orders. "He who knows," he said, "to distinguish between the body and the soul will have no difficulty in perceiving that the spiritual kingdom of Christ and civil government are things very far separated." The State he held to be a Divine institution, to which obedience was due, so far as it restricted itself to the sphere of the outward life. The discipline which he sought to establish in the Church was, in the first instance, successfully resisted. Both the government and the people were opposed to the purity of life which he enforced as a condition of church membership; and he was banished from the Canton. By-and-by he was recalled, for his inestimable services in the community seemed to be indispensable for the preservation of good order; but to the last he was in some respects hindered from establishing a church in entire conformity with his avowed principles.

Nevertheless, his conceptions of church order became the model on which Presbyterian churches generally were organised. That order was confessedly derived solely from the Scriptures, for he held that every church ordinance must have the warrant of Scripture, and that men were under obligation to worship God according to His appointment, and not according to the devices of their own wisdom. Thus, the election of church-officers was vested in the whole body of church members, and these officers consisted exclusively of (1) doctors whose function it was to interpret and expound the Scriptures; (2) pastors, to whom it belonged to preach the Gospel and to administer the Sacraments; then (3) presbyters or elders, who, along with the doctors and pastors, were to conduct the discipline of the Church; and (4) deacons, who were charged with the administration of the charities of the church. This church order was in its whole character and provisions entirely distinct from and independent of the civil government. He did not succeed, however, in preserving intact the respective jurisdictions of Church and State. It has been alleged, indeed, but erroneously, that he made the State subject to the Church. He held that the State ought to be Christian, and, being such, that it was bound to protect and foster the Church, and to listen to its councils; but he did not confound the functions of the magistrate and the church ruler. In this respect only, in common with all the men of his time, did he err, in making heresy punishable by the State, and so virtually in making it obligatory on all citizens to be members of the Church. It may seem strangely inconsistent, yet so it was, that the Reformers, who asserted their freedom against papal tyranny should yet have denied toleration to those who dissented from their creed. They were misled by following the laws of the Jewish theocracy, forgetting that under it a departure from the ordinances of the Church was really treason and rebellion against the sovereign, and therefore punishable. But it was not so in the kingdoms of the world, else no obedience could be due to a heathen government, as the Jews persistently maintained. To make heresy a crime punishable by the State was so far to confound the civil with the ecclesiastical jurisdiction, and therefore Calvin found himself constrained, however reluctantly, to submit to the invasion by the State of the proper province of the Church. He yielded to the assumption by the State of having a potential voice in the nomination of pastors; and the elders of the consistory, which was the supreme tribunal of the Church, were elected by the Council of State.

The Church principles of Calvin obtain perhaps their freest and fullest development in the Reformed Churches of France and of Scotland. Geneva, in the first instance, provided France with ministers, and Calvin and his friends advised the Reformed Church there in every step of its organisation. Its Confession of Faith, adopted in 1559, embraced a church constitution as well as articles of doctrine. That constitution was Presbyterian in form, and the officers whom it recognised were pastors, elders, and deacons. It was professedly founded on Scripture alone, and owed nothing to the State, which was hostile and persecuting. In course of time, under the protection of the Edict of Nantes, this Church enjoyed perfect freedom, and was governed by its own rules of discipline without State interference. Its elders and deacons elected the minister, but care was taken that he should not be intruded upon the people. It had Synods which met twice a year, consisting of all the ministers within the province, and an elder or deacon from each congregation. It decided on questions of appeal, and considered matters affecting the general interests of the Church. It had also a general Synod, consisting of delegates from the provincial Synods of ministers, and of elders and deacons in equal numbers. This organisation was simple, but it was complete, and fitted to serve all the ends of discipline, and to secure freedom without disorder. It stood quite apart from the State, and had nothing to do with civil administration.

The constitution of the Reformed Church of Scotland I reserve for separate and more detailed consideration.

The Church of England was from the first the creature of the State, and to a greater extent, perhaps, than any other Church, has no self-government. The State is the ultimate judge in all causes, civil and ecclesiastical, and the Church has no separate and independent jurisdiction. In its discipline and government it is entirely subject to the State. At the Reformation the king assumed the place of the pope, and exercised all the jurisdiction which the pope claimed; and this servitude of the Church to the temporal sovereign remains intact to this day. It is a servitude which has necessarily proved to be injurious to the well-being both of the Church and of the State. It has also been a perpetual menace to the liberties of the Scottish Church, and was the chief cause in our own day of the entire subversion of these liberties in the State Church.

LECTURE IV.

RELATIONS OF CHURCH AND STATE[1] (*continued*).

It would be interesting to trace the various modifications which were attempted or effected in the relations between Church and State in the various countries of Europe, from the Reformation down to the present century, but such an enquiry would exceed our limits, and carry us too far away from the more immediate scope of these lectures.

The Reformation was a great birth-time of new ideas, and disturbed in many ways the previous relations of society. It was an emancipation from the thraldom which for many centuries had enslaved men in the bonds of ignorance and superstition. To not a few it brought light from heaven, and ushered in the liberty wherewith Christ makes His people free; and to many more it was the starting point of a progress in enlight-

---

[1] For most of the facts contained in this and the preceding Lecture, I am indebted to the work on "Church and State," by Professor Geffckens, translated by E. J. Taylor.

enment which has gone on with accelerated speed to the present day. Especially and immediately, it shook the throne of the papal dominion, which had proved as fatal to morals as it had been to intellectual and political enlargement and liberty. But it abated in no respect the claims of Popery to a universal dominion over all the relations of human life and society. It was not reformed, and its assumptions were such as to make it incapable of reformation. As might have been expected, therefore, it set itself with relentless energy to recover what had been wrested from its cruel grasp. It could no longer, indeed, command the princes and provinces which the Reformation had emancipated, but it might crush them by brute force. Nor were its efforts altogether without success. Protestants were divided in opinion, and were not prepared to offer a combined resistance, but Popery contrived to form a league for their extermination. It is of the essence of the Romish Church to be intolerant. It claims to be the only body which is in the absolute and plenary possession of truth, and refuses to admit that there is truth in any doctrine differing from its own. Every such doctrine is, as its advocates conceive, founded only on ignorance which it must seek to dispel; and, failing in this, the holding of such doctrine becomes a sinful rebellion against infallible authority, and is worthy of death, which is remorselessly inflicted whenever that Church has the power. It would be to abjure its claim to consent to stand on a footing of equality with any other church or religion, and its principles constrain it whenever it has the power to suppress every deviation from its faith, and also all freedom of inquiry and thought which might lead to such a result. It tolerates only what it cannot change, and it claims a sovereignty over kings, whom, when it is able, it employs as its servants to execute its purposes. It was to execute its will that the rising Reformation, which promised such beneficent results, was suppressed in Italy and in Spain. It was to please the Romish Church that the massacre of Protestants in Paris on St. Bartholomew's eve was perpetrated. This was one of the most treacherous and bloody transactions recorded in history, but it was hailed at Rome with jubilant gladness. The Thirty Years'

War, which desolated Germany, had its origin in the same source. It was by a gracious Providence, combined by the patient and dauntless valour, chiefly of the States of Holland, and of Augustus Adolphus of Sweden, that Protestantism was saved from utter extermination. There was no relenting on the part of the Romish Church. In all the countries of Europe where she had the power, she urged on this fatal warfare, and robbed the nations that served her of the best of their people, by compelling them to exile, or by merciless slaughter. It was thus she displayed her mastery, and manifested the principles which swayed her conduct. She asserted for herself a universal dominion over all persons and things, and exercised it wherever it was found possible. And this usurpation has gone very far towards enslaving the Protestant Churches. It tended inevitably to make governments jealous of leaving any power in the hands of the Church, lest she might usurp authority over the State, and invade the secular jurisdiction.

Having experience of the intolerable tyranny of the Romish Church, they deemed it safest to go to the opposite extreme, and to denude the

Church of any separate jurisdiction, even in spiritual matters, and to constitute themselves judges in all causes, civil and ecclesiastical. The Romish Church, moreover, had so confounded and mixed up things sacred and things secular, that it was by no means easy, in that age at least, to distinguish the one from the other. It has often been asserted, that to vindicate the independent spiritual jurisdiction of the Church is to maintain a popish doctrine. It would be much more correct to say, that the domination of the State over the Church is the natural fruit and result of the papal supremacy. Things had been brought to such a pass that there seemed to be no alternative, except either to submit in all things to the domination of the Church, or to enslave it. It seemed impossible otherwise to keep the Church within her legitimate province, and therefore the State assumed the direction of her affairs.

Nay, in these post-reformation days, it became a grave question in Protestant States, whether the Romish Church should be tolerated within their borders. The attitude which it maintained seemed to be such as to make the toleration of it unsafe for the State. It assumed the right of delivering the subjects of Protestant States from their allegiance, by excommunicating their rulers. It was organised as a vast conspiracy against all governments which did not acknowledge the supremacy of the Pope. In England and in Scotland, for example, the very existence of Popery was a great danger. Its priests and people could hardly be regarded otherwise than as conspirators for the overthrow of the Government, and for bringing back the state of things from which these nations had happily escaped, and so of exterminating the Protestant religion, and re-establishing a tyranny which had become intolerable. It seemed not very unreasonable that those who would not tolerate should not be tolerated. Thus it happened that Papists were persecuted, and it has been argued that Protestantism has not proved itself to be more tolerant than Popery. If we charge it against the Romish Church, that its garments are red with the blood of the saints, it is retaliated that Protestant Churches are chargeable with the same crime. Alas, in some measure, it is too true! It was long before the Protestant Churches unlearned the lesson which the Romanists had taught them, and became persuaded that the sword of the magistrate was not the proper instrument for propagating truth, or for suppressing error. The kingdom of Christ is not of this world, and therefore is not to be maintained by the sword. Its weapons are not carnal, but spiritual, and mighty to the pulling down of strongholds.

But to a large extent there were political reasons for what is called the persecution of Romanists. They virtually proclaimed, we and you cannot exist together. Our determined purpose is to destroy you. It was very much in self-defence, therefore, that Romanists were so severely dealt with. They were regarded, and many of them at least were justly regarded, as traitors, and were treated accordingly. It is very true that constructive treason is an extremely dangerous weapon in the hands of a government, and may be, and has been, used as an instrument of cruel oppression. And yet it can hardly be denied that there are conditions of society in which the safety of the commonwealth renders it necessary to employ such a weapon. But, apart from this, history has made it abundantly apparent that, in the hands of Protestants, persecution has been resorted to with reluctance. It is hostile to the spirit of Protestants, and inconsistent with their essential principles, and must therefore, sooner or later, cease. But it is of the very essence of Popery to be intolerant; and it enters upon, and carries forward, the work of persecution, with a zeal and heartiness and thoroughness, which show that it is entirely congenial to its spirit and principles.

My limits do not permit me to detail the various arrangements, by concordats and otherwise, made by the Romish Church with several States after the great struggle of the counter-reformation had exhausted itself; nor is the subject of much importance in its bearing upon our more immediate aim. Neither would it tend much to illustrate the principles which should regulate the relations between Church and State, to examine these relations as they took form in Protestant States, and in reference to Protestant Churches. I must content myself with briefly noticing the state of things as they now exist, as between Church and State, in some of the more important Protestant communities, or in those in which Protestant Churches exist. This state of things will exhibit the results which have been reached after various struggles and modifications.

Before entering upon this, however, I may be permitted, in a few sentences, to advert to two notable events, which, for a time at least, seriously affected the relations between Church and State. I refer to the Protectorate of Cromwell, and to the French Revolution, and the Empire of the First Napoleon. These events were not very remotely connected with each other, and both of them had their source more or less directly in the corruption and tyranny of the Church. Neither of the events had an immediately satisfactory issue, and were of a transitory nature, but they had germs which are bearing fruit to the present day. They were extremely opposite in their character. The one was essentially religious, and the other was anti-religious. The one was a revolt against ecclesiastical tyranny, and the other was a revolt against all institutions in Church and State. In Britain the revolt had ripened before Cromwell had taken a prominent part in it, and seemed tending towards a uniformity of religion under a Presbyterian form of government. Cromwell arrested that movement, and assumed the supreme direction of affairs, both in Church and State. His aim avowedly was to establish a kingdom of God, in which a religious legislature should govern a Church of God-fearing men. He was at variance with the leaders of the earlier movement in two important particulars. He differed from them in their views as to uniformity in religion, and equally so in their views as to the autonomy of the Church. He contended for toleration, and he was an Erastian, as the Congregationalists at that period generally were. He suppressed the Scottish General Assemblies, and by means of agents, called *Triers*, endeavoured over all England to remove scandalous and incompetent ministers, and to replace them by God-fearing and capable men. Church power was wholly merged in the administration of the State. In the hands of Cromwell such administration unquestionably effected a great reformation; and in the state of parties then existing it was not easy, perhaps it was not possible, to devise anything better. But the whole structure collapsed when his strong hand was withdrawn, and that Revolution terminated in the establishment of a more remorseless tyranny than even Laud had initiated.

The French Revolution had wider issues. It shook the thrones of continental Europe, and broke up all pre-existing relations between Church and State, and threatened the extinction of all churches, as well as the overturning of all thrones. Under the military despotism in which it culminated, the relations of Church and State had to be adjusted anew. The power of the Romish Church seemed to be entirely overthrown, and the Pope himself was made a prisoner. But this state of things could not be enduring. The nations could not subsist without a religion, nor be satisfied with the worship of the goddess of reason; and Napoleon was wise enough to see that some terms of adjustment between Church and State must be devised. In France he secured to the Protestants liberty of worship, and this survives to the present day, and forms an enduring monument of the Revolution. Otherwise the relations of Church and State, in France and in other nations, fell to be adjusted anew after the counter-revolution, and may be said to be only now in process of adjustment. Let us see how they stand at present.

A very great and gratifying change is noticeable at this day, as compared with any previous period in European history, inasmuch as now, in all the countries of this great continent, churches have been formed outside those that are established by law, and are entirely free from State control in their administration. A spirit of greater freedom is now pervading the different communities, and a more just apprehension, also, of what is due to the claims of conscience, has brought about this result. It is one pregnant with great issues in the future, and significant of changes which will modify, if not entirely subvert, the relations between States and the Churches which they maintain and control. Many of these non-established churches are of recent formation, and have as yet little or no influence in the countries in which they are tolerated. But, in so far as they are faithful to the truth of Christ, and preach the Gospel of His grace, and administer their affairs in conformity with His will, it is certain that they will grow in strength and influence, and render it impossible for established churches to preserve the exclusive privileges and immunities conferred upon them. In Britain, where they have had longest time to work and to develop their resources, they are already putting in peril even the existence of the Established Churches, and have stripped them of many of the immunities they once enjoyed. In England, church rates have been abolished, and the gates of the great universities have been opened to Nonconformists, and all places and offices are as open to Dissenters as to Churchmen. In Scotland the Established Church has been deprived of its control over parochial schools, and Dissenters are eligible to the chairs of its universities. The question is raised and agitated, Whether the establishing and endowing a church is a legitimate method of maintaining and propagating religion; and even if it were, whether by such a method religion is not rather hindered and hampered? Whether the well-being of a community is promoted by Church Establishment and Endowment; and consequently, whether a State is justified in spending its revenues in this way? Whether the essential freedom of the Church is compatible with its endowment by the State; and, if not, whether it is not greatly better to have no Established Church than to have it in a state of bondage? Whether the Church which realises the Headship of Christ, and consequently her obligation to act out His will in all things, as He may give her light and direction, is more powerful and influential in the promotion of His cause, than when hampered by State enactments, and burdened with State endowments? Whether a Church which keeps her eye singly directed to Christ, and is thus brought into closer fellowship with Him, is not a more effective instrument for preserving and diffusing the truth, than when her eye is necessarily somewhat diverted to State enactments? These are questions awaiting their solution in this and in other lands. But however they may be determined, even should it appear in the light of Scripture and of history that, in certain circumstances, it is lawful and expedient for the State to establish and endow the Church, this appears certain, that it is better unspeakably to have no Established Church than to have a Church so fettered by State enactments that she is not free to carry into effect the will of her great King and Lawgiver.

It cannot be regarded as a satisfactory solution of the questions affecting the relations of Church and State, to say that the State should take nothing to do with religion; that it should assume an attitude of entire indifference, and regard with equal complacency or disfavour the Christian and the Atheist. If this were even desirable—which it is not—it is impossible. The governing body in a State is composed of individuals, none of whom is, or can be, indifferent to religion. He that is not for it is against it. He must either yield to its claims or reject them. In the latter case he cannot regard religion with complacency; and will probably, as at the first French Revolution, use his endeavours to suppress it, because he regards it as hostile to the well-being of the commonwealth. If he accepts, say, the Christian religion, he cannot be a party to measures which would be subversive of it. He may and ought to see to it, that no citizen is made to suffer in his person and property on account of his religion; that, whatever his religious views may be, his rights as a citizen shall be conserved, unless, indeed, he professes principles which are inconsistent with the safety of the State. But a legislator acting in this spirit may be persuaded that, as regards all the interests of the community over which he rules, it is best that they should be Christians; that their being Christians would be the best security for their being loyal, and intelligent, and peaceable subjects, rendering obedience to the law for conscience' sake. In such a case he could not surely be blameable if, as a statesman, he did what he could to maintain and promote Christianity within the borders of his dominion. It may be difficult enough, indeed, for him to determine what he can do in this direction. It may be the best thing he can do to leave the church or churches unaided and free to do their proper work in Christianising the people, at the same time taking care that his legislation shall not hamper or hinder them in it. If there are various denominations in the country, all doing good Christian work, it would be politically unjust that he should establish and endow one of them at the expense of all the rest; and it may be a fair question for him always, whether, by the endowment of one or more of them, he is not hindering rather than promoting the moral, social, and religious interests of the people? The establishment and endowment of a church can only be vindicated on the ground that by so doing the well-being of the community is better secured; and this can only be permanently effected when no injustice is done to any party, and when the Church at the same time is left unfettered to do what the law of Christ renders obligatory upon her. Looking at the condition of the nations of Europe at this time, it would be very difficult to point to one of them in which a Church could be established on such conditions. The progress of events seems rather to indicate that the time is not far distant when Established Churches will cease to be. When that time comes it will not necessarily follow that States shall cease to be Christian, and when the laws they enact and enforce shall not be in harmony with Christian truth and be bulwarks for its defence. But if this is to be, it can only be by leavening the minds of the people with Christian principles; and to this end the churches meanwhile should put forth every effort, in the name of Christ, and by His gracious power,—healing the sore diseases o the community, casting out devils, and quickening the dead. If they fail in this, no doubt a dark time is coming, when the kingdoms will be surrendered to the power either of Popery or of Atheism. Both of these are striving for the mastery with a new-born energy, and they can only be resisted and overcome by the Gospel of the grace of God. This is the one weapon which is mighty to the pulling down of strongholds.

When we say that the Christianity of a State is not necessarily bound up with the establishment of a Church, we do not speak theoretically or conjecturally. It is not only possible, in the nature of the case, but in the United States of America we have actually one of the most powerful States of the world, which has not ceased to be Christian, although for generations it has had no Established Church. It may be, indeed, that all the members of its Legislature are not Christians; but its Congress and Senate meet under invocation of the name of Christ, and by formally asking His direction and blessing. The Government appoint chaplains for this purpose, who at every sitting open the meeting with prayer. They also appoint military chaplains for the army and navy; and even when not on service sailors are under obligation to attend Divine worship. It openly professes to be a Christian State, and provides for the religious instruction of its own servants. Its legislation aims at being in harmony with Christian ordinances, and it shields the churches in the peaceable observance of their worship. It does not intermeddle with their administration, unless in regard to civil rights, and to prevent any outrage on morality. So much does it assume the Christian character, and proceed on the assumption that it is Christian, that a will made in favour of a society of Atheists was annulled by the Supreme Court of Justice in Pennsylvania, on the ground that the law of the State recognised no societies but such as were religious, charitable, or literary. In all the States the observance of the Sabbath is protected by law, that worship in the churches may not be disturbed; and religious fasts and thanksgiving days are appointed by the State. Places of worship are exempted from taxation, and in most of the States ministers of the Gospel are exempted from military service. Polygamy and adultery are punishable as crimes. The non-existence of an Established Church is far from indicating any indifference to religion on the part either of the Government or the people. Nowhere are the liberties of the Church more jealously guarded, and nowhere is religious zeal more energetic. It is almost universally felt that Christianity is an immense social power, without whose influence the nation would be deprived of its strength, and sink into moral and political decay. Like almost all the European nations, the United States are beginning to experience the difficulty of dealing with the Romish population, chiefly as regards the matter of the education of the young. Largely, by a constant flow of immigration from Ireland, the Romish Church has become a great power in the State; and its adherents boldly express the hope that, ere long, they will be able to secure the election of a president of their own creed. To a large extent they have withdrawn their children from the public schools, because these do not provide instruction in the doctrines of their Church, and are organising parochial schools of their own. But this movement on their part has awakened the zeal of Protestant denominations, who, feeling that this popish endeavour cannot be successfully met by a merely secular school system, are aiming, with good prospects of success, at the establishment of schools which shall be at once Christian and unsectarian.

Except in Great Britain, where the Romish Church is making such progress, and gaining such power and influence as to create serious alarm in many quarters, it has lost the commanding position it recently occupied in many of the countries of Europe, and its relations with the State have been materially changed. It has ceased to control and direct the policy of the kingdoms in which its authority was once absolute. No Government is now obedient to its dictates. Its pretensions and claims were never so high as at the present time, and it never was so destitute of power to vindicate and maintain them. The fact that the Pope has ceased to be a temporal sovereign, does not, perhaps, materially detract from the spiritual authority which he wields over the members of the Romish Church; but he is no longer a member of the comity of nations, and has no direct political influence. In his present position he is a great practical solecism. Without abandoning some of his pretensions, he cannot be a subject of any Government, and he has no territory in which to exercise royal authority, except within the limits of the Vatican, which is secured to him by a guarantee which he repudiates.

It is in Italy, as might be assumed, that the greatest change has been effected in the relations of Church and State, by the revolution which happily united in one kingdom the whole Italian territory. The Government have steadily carried out the great conception of Cavour of a free Church in a free State. Consequently all Italy, including Rome, is now open to the Gospel; and the Waldenses, long shut up within their valleys, are spreading their evangelistic agencies over the land; while various other denominations are also diffusing, not without success, the light of the Gospel. The Romish Church is also entirely free to prosecute its work, though its relation to the State has been entirely changed. The king, who is under the ban of excommunication, is excluded from the exercise of secular compulsion for carrying into effect any ecclesiastical measures; but, on the other hand, he is debarred from interfering to prevent compliance with them. To the Pope is granted a country residence, and the free enjoyment of the Vatican and its precincts, which are exempted from the jurisdiction of the State. His person is declared inviolable, and the honours of a sovereign are awarded to him, with a pension which he refuses to accept and has characterised as Judas money. His spiritual jurisdiction and authority, without interference by the civil power, is fully conserved to him; and there is no appeal to the Civil Courts in matters pertaining to ecclesiastical affairs. The institutions in Rome founded for the education of the clergy are left dependent on the Pope, without interference by the Government in their educational department. Ecclesiastical assemblies of any kind are free to meet without permission of the Crown. The ecclesiastical authorities have the power of nomination to all ecclesiastical appointments, subject to the proviso that notice of their nomination be given to the Government; and that, to entitle them to the temporalities, the nominees must be Italian subjects. The communal authorities have the charge of registration, and the Church is deprived of all compulsory power in regard to baptisms, marriages, and burials. Conventual establishments no longer enjoy the privileges of corporate bodies, and their property has been transferred to the State, subject to the provision of a pension to the members. They now occupy the position of voluntary associations, and their members may leave them if they choose. It is perhaps needless to enter further into detail. No doubt the conception of Cavour of a free Church in a free State has been to a very large extent realised by the Italian Government; and one cannot fail to admire the wisdom with which, in circumstances of extreme difficulty, they have peaceably placed things on their present footing, in spite of the most formidable anathemas and denunciations of the papal authorities.

In 1867-8 Austria began to emancipate herself from the thraldom of Rome. At that time laws declared to be fundamental were enacted, declaring the equality of all subjects before the law, liberty of faith, and freedom of conscience, the exercise of civil and political rights irrespective of creeds, and the supervision of education by the State. These laws encountered, of course, the determined opposition of the Romish Church, and, in consequence of a reactionary policy, were for a time not very faithfully executed. Protestant worship, though not prohibited, was conducted under painful police supervision. Though nominally possessing equal rights with the Romanists, Protestants were not allowed to meet in congregation, and much less in Synod or Presbytery, without the permission and presence of the police. In Hungary this treatment was vehemently opposed; and, under fear of a revolution, full freedom of worship was finally secured for the Protestants. To the Romish Church, deprived of much of the power it had hitherto exercised, was granted the free exercise of her constitution, so far as regards purely ecclesiastical jurisdiction and discipline, the management and development of her institutions, the regulation of clerical education, the direction of her schools and seminaries, and of religious instruction in public schools, and the administration of ecclesiastical property. These laws are far from being so thorough and revolutionary as those of Italy, but they go a good way in restricting the domination of Romanism. The jurisdiction of the Church is strictly limited within her own sphere, and is upheld only by her own instruments of authority, and official power is not employed in enforcing obedience to her mandates. The State has also reserved to itself the exclusive right of control in regard to monastic and conventual establishments. No new order can be established without the consent of the Government, and entrance into orders is made dependent on the legal consent of the family; while every person also is left free to leave the society, and to have the property restored to him which he brought into it, religious vows having no civil obligation. Testamentary bequests to such communities, moreover, require the sanction of the State. So stands the law in Austria, in spite of papal and clerical opposition. Both in that empire and in Italy there is pervading the whole legislation a distinct recognition of the autonomy of the Church, and of its separate and independent jurisdiction; and this has gone very far to secure a comparatively peaceful and probably enduring settlement in both countries, pregnant with very hopeful issues for the future.

Even Spain has ceased to yield the abject submission to papal decrees which so long degraded and weakened her. Liberty of religious worship was formally sanctioned by the constitution of 1869, and was confirmed on the accession of the late king in 1875. Of this the Pope complained as an infringement of treaties, and ominous of evil for the nation. The liberty is indeed of a very restricted kind. Protestants are forbidden to give any public notice of their services by placard or otherwise, and the doors of their churches must be kept closed during public worship. But even such restricted liberty is full of alarm to papal authorities, and one of its bishops fulminates an excommunication against all who sit at meat with heretics, or look kindly on them; against every person who lets a house to them for worship, or who gives them money, or leaves a legacy to them; against every one who lives on terms of friendship with them, or speaks or writes a word in their defence. Protestantism will live and grow in spite of such fulminations, and Popery may begin to learn that these weapons are by no means the most powerful she can employ in winning or retaining the allegiance of men.

In France and Belgium the question as to the

relations between Church and State hinges chiefly on the matter of education, and in neither of these countries is it quite definitely determined in whose hands the control of education should be. In both, the Romish Church claims it, and the Governments seem to be unable to wrest it out of their hands. The great mass of the population are Romanists, and the priesthood there, as elsewhere, exercise over them an almost unlimited sway. In both countries, however, there is freedom of worship, of which Protestants avail themselves. In Belgium, the Protestant cause is weak, although its adherents are zealous, and by laudable evangelistic enterprise are extending their influence. In France, the Protestant Church takes rank as an Establishment, but is largely under the control of the State. It has virtually no Confession of Faith, and consequently no power of discipline. It is, however, growing in purity of doctrine, and is aiming, not without hope of success, at the restoration of its old creed, and the reassertion of the freedom it enjoyed at the period of the Reformation. Outside the Established Church, the evangelical union and other agencies are widely diffusing

Gospel truth, and few countries at present afford a more hopeful field for evangelistic labour; all the more, perhaps, because the Romish Church has not only ceased from the assertion of its Gallican liberties, but has degenerated into the grossest superstitions and pure Mariolatry.

There is no country in Europe in which the relations of Church and State are in a condition more unsatisfactory than in the cantons of Switzerland. Though republican in form, and though the population exercises a very direct control in the government, the churches, both Romish and Protestant, are subjected to a tyrannical Erastian sway. Infidelity is largely prevalent, and there, as everywhere, is bitterly hostile to religion, and represses its free exercise and the enforcement of its discipline.

In Germany the relations of Church and State are very far from being satisfactory. The Governments, in its different provinces, have concerned themselves very much with the adjustment of these relations, and largely, perhaps on that account, have failed in arriving at a satisfactory result. Apparently they have never been able to perceive that the Church is not a proper field for the exercise of civil jurisdiction. I cannot enter into detail as to various modifications which from time to time have been effected in the different States in regard to the government of the Church, and proceed at once to a brief review of what have been designated the Falk laws, which exhibit the present attitude of the German empire toward the churches established within its border. The design of these laws was to repress and limit the exorbitant and dangerous powers which were exercised by Romish ecclesiastics; and so far the design was laudable, and seemed even to be necessary. But in that case they should have been limited in their operation to the Romish Church, from which alone the danger was apprehended. They were, however, made applicable universally to all churches receiving State pay. This indeed might have been equitable enough, if care had been taken to distinguish between the civil and ecclesiastical province in regard to all churches alike. Unhappily the Falk laws have, in several respects, invaded the ecclesiastical province, and inflict a real grievance both upon the Romish and Protestant Churches. This seems the more inexcusable, as the German Government had the example, to guide them to a wiser course of both Italy and Austria. By not following this example Prussia has involved itself in a conflict with the Romish Church of very doubtful issue. Since the passing of these laws several additional enactments have been found necessary; but they have all proceeded on the same assumptions, and have not tended to bring about a better order of things. By these laws a supreme court for ecclesiastical causes is established, consisting of eleven lay members, six of whom must be judges, to decide finally on all church questions. Its jurisdiction can be invoked by any ecclesiastic who has been deprived of office; and if his appeal is sustained, the court has power to annul the ecclesiastical sentence, and to compel the church authorities to withdraw it, under heavy penalties, and to suspend them from office. Such a law strikes at the root of all ecclesiastical discipline, and is obnoxious alike to both Romanist and Protestant. It is reasonable enough that an appeal should lie to such a tribunal as to whether an ecclesiastic who has been deprived of office should in consequence lose the emoluments pertaining to it, but no civil tribunal can have the right to retain him in his office, if the Church is to have any spiritual jurisdiction at all. The Falk laws commit the same fatal error in some of their provisions regarding the training and appointment of ecclesiastics. It is right enough in the State to enact that ecclesiastics who receive its pay should possess certain scholarly qualifications, but the Church must be left free to prescribe and to judge of their theological instruction; and whatever power of nomination the State may exercise, it is only by the co-operation of the Church that ecclesiastics can be inducted to their office. In the conflict to which these laws have given birth Prussia has not been honoured with much success, and is beginning to find that laws become a dead letter when they outrage the common sentiment and convictions of the people who are subject to them. It is not by such weapons that Romanism is to be suppressed. Germany needs yet to learn the lesson which Luther taught her long ago, that you cannot strike a spirit with the sword.

LECTURE V.

RELATION OF CHURCH AND STATE IN SCOTLAND.

In severing her connection with the State in 1843, the Free Church asserted her claim to be recognised as the true Church of Scotland, not the less because she had ceased to be the Established Church. This she did in the Claim of Right adopted by the General Assembly 1842, with the view of being submitted to the Legislature. It was an appeal to Parliament to deliver the Church from the invasion by the Civil Courts of her rightful jurisdiction, which she believed had been secured to her by various Statutes, and which, in any event, she could not as a Church of Christ cease to assert and maintain, whether in connection with the State or separated from it. The refusal by the Legislature to sustain this claim of the Church, and thereby the virtual affirmation by the State of the judgments of the Civil Courts, by which her jurisdiction was undermined and overthrown, did not alter the character of the claim, nor falsify the assertion that the Church which maintained such jurisdiction was the Church hitherto recognised as the Church of Scotland. The claim to be such is set forth in general terms as follows:—

"The General Assembly, while they fully recognise the absolute jurisdiction of the Civil Courts in relation to all matters whatsoever of a civil nature, and especially in relation to all the temporalities conferred by the State upon the Church, and the civil consequences attached by law to the decisions in matters spiritual of the Church Courts—do, in name and on behalf of the Church, and of the nation and people of Scotland, and under the sanction of the several Statutes, and the Treaty of Union hereinbefore recited, claim as of right that she shall freely possess and enjoy her liberties, government, discipline, rights, and privileges, according to law, especially for the defence of the spiritual liberties of her people, and that she shall be protected therein from the foresaid unconstitutional and illegal encroachments of the Court of Session, and her people secured in their Christian and constitutional rights and liberties.

"And they declare that they cannot, in accordance with the Word of God, and authorised and ratified Standards of this Church, and the dictates of their consciences, intrude ministers on reclaiming congregations, or carry on the government of Christ's Church, subject to the coercion attempted by the Court of Session; and at the risk and hazard of suffering the loss of the secular benefits conferred by the State, and the public advantages of an Establishment, they must, as by God's grace they will, refuse so to do; for highly as they estimate these, they cannot put them in competition with the inalienable liberties of a Church of Christ, which, alike by their duty and allegiance to their Head and King, and by their ordination vows, they are bound to maintain, notwithstanding of whatsoever trouble or persecution may arise.

"And they protest that all and whatsoever Acts of the Parliament of Great Britain passed without the consent of this Church and nation in alteration of, or derogation to the government, discipline, rights, and privileges of this Church; as also all and whatsoever sentences of Courts, in contravention of the same government, discipline, rights, and privileges are, and shall be in themselves, null and void, and of no legal force and effect; and that, while they will accord full submission to all such acts and sentences, in so far—though in so far only—as these may regard civil rights and privileges, whatever may be their opinion of the justice or legality of the same, their said submission shall not be deemed an acquiescence therein, but that it shall be free to the members of this Church, or their successors at any time hereafter, when there shall be a prospect of obtaining justice, to claim the restitution of all such civil rights and privileges, and temporal benefits and endowments, as for the present they may be compelled to yield up, in order to preserve to their office-bearers the free exercise of their spiritual government and discipline, and to their people the liberties of which respectively it has been attempted, so contrary to law and justice, to deprive them.[1]

"And finally, the General Assembly invite all

---

[1] This protestation is grounded on the Treaty of Union, according to which the rights and privileges of the Church of Scotland were reserved from the cognisance and power of the federal Legislature which the Union created.

the office-bearers and members of this Church, who are willing to suffer for their allegiance to their adorable King and Head, to stand by the Church, and by each other, in defence of the doctrines aforesaid, and of the liberties and privileges, whether of office-bearers or people, which rest upon it; and to unite in supplication to Almighty God, that He would be pleased to turn the hearts of the rulers of this kingdom to keep unbroken the faith pledged to this Church in former days by Statutes and solemn treaty, and the obligations come under to God Himself, and to preserve and maintain the government and discipline of this Church in accordance with His Word."

In terms equally clear and emphatic in the Protest on 18th May 1843, when she relinquished her Establishment, the Free Church asserted this claim. The Protest says—"Considering that while heretofore, as members of Church judicatories ratified by law and recognised by the constitution of this kingdom, we hold ourselves entitled and bound to exercise and maintain this jurisdiction vested in these judicatories with the sanction of the constitution, notwithstanding the decrees as to matters spiritual and ecclesiastical of the Civil Courts, because we could not see that the State had required submission thereto as a condition of the Establishment; but, on the contrary, were satisfied that the State, by the Acts of the Parliament of Scotland for ever and unalterably secured to this nation by the Treaty of Union, had repudiated any power in the Civil Courts to pronounce such decrees, we are now constrained to acknowledge it to be the mind and will of the State, as recently declared, that such submission should and does form a condition of the Establishment, and of the possession of the benefits thereof; and that as we cannot, without committing what we believe to be sin—in opposition to God's law, in disregard of the honour and authority of Christ's Crown, and in violation of our own solemn vows—comply with this condition, we cannot in conscience continue connected with it, and retain the benefits of an Establishment to which such condition is attached.

"We, therefore, the ministers and elders foresaid, on this the first occasion since the rejection by the Legislature of the Church's Claim of Right, when the commissioners chosen from throughout the bounds of the Church to the General Assembly appointed to have been this day holden, are convened together, do protest, that the conditions foresaid, while we deem them contrary to, and subversive of, the settlement of Church government effected at the Revolution, and solemnly guaranteed by the Act of Security and Treaty of Union, are also at variance with God's Word, in opposition to the doctrines and fundamental principles of the Church of Scotland, inconsistent with the freedom essential to the right constitution of a Church of Christ, and incompatible with the government which He, as the Head of His Church, hath therein appointed, distinct from the civil magistrate.

"And we further protest, that any Assembly constituted in submission to the conditions now declared to be law, and under the civil coercion which has been brought to bear on the election of commissioners to this Assembly, this day appointed to have been holden, and on the commissioners chosen thereto, is not, and shall not, be deemed a lawful and free Assembly of the Church of Scotland, according to the original and fundamental principles thereof."

These are very strong assertions, made both in the Claim of Right and in the Protest, and I have quoted them at some length, that their import might be clearly apparent; for, although both the documents are public and easy of access, and both in substance and form were very fully in the minds of the past generation, yet, after the lapse of more than forty years, and in the progress of events, they have largely passed into oblivion, and members of the Free Church, as well as others, are not alive to what they contain, and to the relation which they set forth as existing between the Church now established in Scotland and the State which established it.

The allegations contained in these documents are, it may be fairly admitted, antecedently improbable, and many would be disposed to regard them *prima facie* as groundless. It is, in the first place, unlikely that Civil Courts, the judges in which are trained and accustomed to interpret and apply Acts of legislation, should have so misunderstood and misapplied the Acts in relation to the Church of Scotland, as to overthrow the legal rights and privileges of that

Church. And, secondly, it is improbable that, if they had done so, the Imperial Legislature would have refused to redress the wrong. Yet it must be admitted that both of these things are possible. It is possible that judges, under the blinding influence of prejudice, may misinterpret the laws they are appointed to administer. And it is possible that the Legislature may refuse redress, because, in their view, a Free Church, whose ministers are salaried by the State, is pregnant with danger, and ought to be in subjection to the Civil Government in all causes, ecclesiastical as well as civil.

On the other hand, one may surely be permitted to say, that it is in a very high degree improbable that the General Assembly, which asserted the Claim of Right, and those who subscribed the Protest, could be mistaken in averring that the law had been so misinterpreted and misapplied. For they were not ignorant fanatics who, having conceived certain airy notions of what a Church of Christ ought to be, in defiance of all law and precedent, determined to carry their views into effect. Their number included men who were confessedly the flower of

Scottish intelligence and integrity, several of them lawyers of high distinction, and not likely to be mistaken in their apprehension of the liberties which had been secured to the Church—men conversant with history, and habituated to the administration of affairs. And yet they have not hesitated to aver that the Court of Session did invade the lawful jurisdiction of the Church, and that to such an extent as entirely to extinguish it. And this they did, in spite of all temporal inducements to the contrary, in the certainty that by acting upon their convictions they would sustain the loss of what they greatly valued—ministers, the loss of all they had in the world, and others, the loss of the public advantage of an Establishment, which they regarded as in many ways of great importance for the well-being of the community. It was far from being in a revolutionary spirit that they so acted as men determined on the establishment of a new order of things—reformers of what had become antiquated, and no longer suitable for present exigencies. On the contrary, they were religiously conservative—resolute to walk in the old paths, and to maintain the old landmarks. They aimed at establishing nothing new. They regarded the immunities of the Church as a glorious inheritance, into the possession of which they had entered, and they did what they could to preserve them intact, notwithstanding of whatever trouble or persecution might arise. The Church, whose liberties they defended, was, as they firmly believed and proved, the Church which Knox had been mainly instrumental in organising, and which their fathers had shed their blood in defending.

It should be kept in remembrance, also, that the judges of the Court of Session were by no means unanimous in their judgment as to the question of law, or as to the competency of the Court to determine the matters submitted to them. It was by a somewhat narrow majority that the Court committed the fatal blunder of invading the proper province of the Church, and the minority of the judges were certainly the most eminent among them for clear-sighted intelligence. We are not at all disposed to question the perfect integrity of any of the judges in the case; but the majority, we may fairly say, were not far-sighted enough to perceive what was really involved in the judgments they gave, although, at the first, Lord Cockburn gave them a somewhat emphatic warning. He said—"It is the duty of a Supreme Court to avoid every collision through which it cannot see its way. Its dignity must necessarily be put into jeopardy by its exposing itself to a conflict in which it cannot explain how it is to prevail. This I fear is the position in which the Court is about to place itself. It is about to enter upon an untried voyage, without star or compass. No one, either of the bar or of the bench, can tell us what is to come next."

There were influences at work, besides, which were fitted to disturb the vision of these judges, and which doubtless operated on their minds. The question of jurisdiction was raised under the Act of the General Assembly on Calls, under which Presbyteries were instructed to arrest any proceedings towards the settlement of a minister, if the majority of heads of families in a congregation objected to him, as not fitted to edify them. We shall have occasion hereafter more particularly to examine this Act, and its relation to the antecedent history of the Church; but we refer to it in the present connection for the purpose of saying, that its manifest object being to defend the members of the Church against the intrusion of unacceptable ministers, it could hardly fail in being peculiarly obnoxious to a certain class in the community, who were scared into a feeling of strong resentment and dread apprehension by the democratic character of the Reform Bill, so recently enacted. At that time everything conceded to the people in the way of franchise, or any power entrusted to them, was regarded by this class as in a high degree dangerous to the constitution of the country. This Act of Assembly seemed to be of such a character, and for this reason was fitted to create in certain minds a strong prejudice against it; and judges, not less than other men, are liable to be influenced by the currents of feeling and opinion that are prevalent in society.

Besides, the Act of Assembly on Calls was a recent thing in the *practice* of the Church, and to those who were not very conversant with its history, might very readily appear to be an unwarrantable innovation. Under the long and dreary reign of Moderatism, extending over nearly one hundred years, the Church had made no difficulty about intruding unacceptable ministers, no matter how strong the opposition of the people might be. During all that time, indeed, the form of a call was still adhered to; but it was treated as of no force or efficacy whatever. It was regarded as a formal ceremony handed down by tradition from the fathers, and an utterly insignificant element in the settlement of a minister. The Assembly's Act on Calls completely changed all that, and gave the congregation a place and power in this matter—a matter which more deeply concerned them than it did any other party. There was, however, a powerful section of the Church who were strongly opposed to the restoration of the ancient privileges of the congregation; and this section had the entire sympathy of many outside the Church of Scotland, who, on the one hand, regarded with extreme jealousy and dislike anything which was fitted to advance the interests of evangelical religion; or who, on the other hand, belonged to churches in which the views and feelings of church members were of no account.

In these circumstances, it was not very surprising that even such men as the majority of the judges in the Court of Session should unconsciously have had their minds warped and prejudiced so as to lead to a miscarriage of law in the Auchterarder Case, and which led to an equal miscarriage in many other cases in relation to the Church adjudicated upon at the time.

It ought to be kept in view also, that their judgment did not rest solely on the Statutes which they interpreted and applied, but on certain considerations of a general character, which were stated both at the bar and from the bench. For example, it was urged that there is no wrong without a remedy; and as it appeared to them that both the presentee and the patron had suffered wrong by the refusal to induct Mr. Young as minister of Auchterarder, it belonged to the Court of Session to rectify that wrong. This implied two assumptions, both of which are alike untenable. There are many wrongs which admit of no human remedy; and were it not so, it is absurd to say that it is the province of the Court of Session to rectify all wrongs. It was urged that "there must be some court or other judicature by which every other court or judicature may be either compelled to do their duty, or kept within the bounds of their own duty;" and it was assumed that this was the prerogative of the Court of Session, although in the Statutes constituting the Court its jurisdiction is expressly limited to civil matters. This other ground for interference was also alleged, that as the refusal to induct the presentee involved civil consequences, the Court had a right to interfere. But this implies their right to interfere in the whole discipline of the Church; for it is difficult to conceive of a case in which such discipline may not affect, more or less, the temporal interests of the person upon whom it is exercised.

But then what is to be said of the judgment of the House of Lords, to which the first Auchterarder Case was appealed? They affirmed the judgment of the Court of Session, and it cannot be assumed that their judgment was swayed by the same bias as might have influenced the Scottish judges. But it is really easier to account for their judgment than for that of the Scottish judges. It proceeded on the assumption that the only bar to the induction of a presentee was that the Presbytery should find him deficient in literary attainment, or that there was some stain upon his moral character, or that his doctrine was not in accordance with the Confession of Faith. They ridiculed the idea of the congregation having anything to say in the matter, and it seems inconceivable to an English mind that Church Courts should have any distinct and independent jurisdiction. This, then, was the law as declared by the House of Lords. No valid objection could lie against the induction of a presentee, except what related to his doctrine, life, or literature. And yet, within a very few years thereafter, the same House, acting not in its judicial, but in its legislative capacity, passed a declaratory law that objections of any kind relating to the fitness of the presentee for the particular parish were admissible, and might, if proved, bar his induction. Thus what the judicial Lords had found to be law was declared by the Legislature not to be law. It was in vain that the judges protested that such a declaration of law was inconsistent with their finding in the Auchterarder case; and that their finding must have been different, if they had believed that what was now proposed to be declared as law had really been the law. Such a fiasco has perhaps seldom occurred in the history of legislation and the administration of law. Surely our fathers acted wisely in seeking to provide, by the Act of Security accompanying the Treaty of Union, that the British Legislature should be precluded from intermeddling with the Scottish Church. And yet that Act has proved an insufficient protection. It was flagrantly violated within five years after its enactment, and might as well have been non-existent.

Intelligent observers outside the Church, of very various opinions otherwise, had no difficulty in declaring that those who were constrained to sever their connection with the State, by the refusal of the Legislature to sustain their Claim of Right, and to defend them from the action of the Civil Courts, by which the whole sphere of the Church's jurisdiction was invaded, were the real inheritors and representatives of the Church of the Reformation. Thus Lord Jeffrey, as stated in his *Life* by Lord Cockburn, held that "honest men could do nothing but leave it" (the Church as now established); and the heroism with which this was done made him proud of his country. His view was "that the Church of Scotland, which had owed its existence to its defiance of the Civil Supremacy that had been claimed by the Stuarts, had been revived when the Stuarts were put down, as it had been originally founded on the very principle of its independence in spiritual matters; that in the modern conflict it was demanding nothing but what had immemorially been assumed in practice, and even in judicial practice, to be its right; that, instead of implying ecclesiastical tyranny, the system had worked so well, that there never was a Church better fitted for the people, or to which the people were more attached."

In the same spirit Lord Macaulay has said, "Suppose that we could call up from the grave the Presbyterian Divines who then sat in the General Assembly (1707); suppose that we could call up Carstairs; that we could call up Boston, the author of the *Fourfold State;* that we could relate to them the history of the ecclesiastical revolutions which have since their time taken place in Scotland; and that we could then ask them, Is the Established Church, or is the Free Church, identical with the Church that existed at the time of the Union?—Is it not quite certain what their answer would be? They would say, Our Church, the Church which you promised to maintain unalterable, was not the Church which you protect, but the Church which you oppress. Our Church was the Church of Chalmers and Brewster, not the Church of Bryce and Muir."

In a Letter to a Free Church elder, immediately subsequent to the Disruption, Mr. Fraser Tytler, the Scottish historian, says, "I don't see how, consistently with your principles and belief in what constitutes a true Presbyterian Kirk, you could have acted otherwise; had I been a Presbyterian I would have done the same. Popular election of their ministers, and complete spiritual independence, were, from the first, the two great principles laid down by Knox as the foundation on which their whole superstructure rested; and indeed without the last no Church could stand."

In a speech in the House of Commons in 1874, Mr. Gladstone said, "I am not able to avoid giving my opinion on the subject. I was one of a number, now very small, who watched with much interest the progress of the controversy which began in 1834 and ended in 1843; and I did not at that time scruple to state in print my opinion that, so far as the traditions and principles of the original Scotch Reformation were concerned, the Free Church, or rather those who afterwards became the Free Church, whatever might be the compatibility, or the reverse, of their views with National Establishment, were certainly the heirs of the principles, theological and ecclesiastical, that are connected with the Scotch Reformation."

Not less important and significant was the testimony borne by deputies from various churches who appeared at the General Assemblies of the Free Church in Edinburgh, in May 1843, and in Glasgow, in October of the same year. As, for example, the representatives from the Presbyterian Church in Ireland, who had been deputed to the as yet undisrupted Church, laid their commission on the table of the Free Church Assembly, and not on that of the remanent Establishment, with this expression of opinion: "It has been asked, why we table our commission here? We are sent with a commission to appear before the Church of our fathers—why have we tabled that commission here? I say that we were bound, after having examined all the circumstances as they appeared to us, to regard this Assembly as the representative of the Church of our fathers. We come here to the Presbyterian Church of Scotland, and we confess that, after examination, we are not able to acknowledge and to recognise as the true Presbyterian Church a body of men who submit to be controlled, and to be ruled, and to be governed, by any number of men without the Church, and who have no place and no part in the Church."

To the same effect is the testimony of the Synod of United Original Seceders. "These principles (the principles maintained by the Free Church) involve the honour of Christ as King of Zion. You have asserted them within His own house—you have contended for the liberty with which Christ makes His people free—and you have secured that liberty for the members of Christ's Church. The principles for which you have been contending are the principles of the Confession of Faith and the Standards of the Church, for which our forefathers contended—for which they were persecuted and suffered as you have been."

In somewhat similar terms spoke all the numerous deputies to the Assembly in 1843.

A testimony of a like kind, and not less valuable, was borne by one who was not a deputy to the Assembly, but an intelligent observer of what had taken place, who had taken pains to investigate the whole matter at issue, and published his views upon it, and the grounds of them, in a volume which should not be allowed to fall into oblivion. I refer to the Reverend Adolphus Sydow, a distinguished Prussian minister, and chaplain to the Court at Potsdam, who was in this country at the time of the Disruption. Mr Sydow says—" In Scotland matters have stood, and do stand, in a position quite different from that in other Protestant countries—different, not as has been so frequently and unfairly objected, because of the wilful obstinacy of a puritanical zealotism—not because of a crafty agitation striving to use, for foreign and selfish purposes, the deep love which every Scotchman entertains for his Church; nor because of the systematic operation of an ambitious and power-loving clergy; but different, because of statute laws and liberties of the Church acknowledged by the State itself. Scotland is that spot on earth where Providence has introduced into history the germs of sound principle in the relations of Church and State, and the English Government has received from the hand of God the honour and the conditions to give free action to these principles. The spirit of the Scotch Church, which has come forth out of all its conflicts since the Reformation, one and the same, uncoerced and untrammelled, is no vague unknown thing against which the State has always to be suspiciously on its guard; on the contrary, it is plain and intelligible to every one acquainted with her history. There is nothing in this spirit that would prevent a Government from exercising all just and becoming authority, and the movement of the Scottish Church about the year 1834 was in reality, not a movement against the State, but a movement within her own body. . . . The Scottish Church has in her constitution a clearly-defined position as regards the State, which she, as long as she will remain an Establishment, for her part, would have no right to alter, and which, in fact, she did not feel tempted to alter in the year 1834; but, on the other hand, she would scarcely allow the same to be altered by mere pressure from without. The spirit of the Scottish Church plainly put forth by her recognised Standards, and again preserving these Standards with watchful care and zeal, clear and effective in organisation and discipline, beyond anything the author has seen in other Protestant Communions—penetrating into the inmost core of the national life and character—is that right of the Church which is recognised in the pages of history, and legalised by statutory law. From the date of the Union of both kingdoms, up to the present time, it had never been openly declared by the State, that this spirit is inconsistent with the essential conditions of an Establishment, nor is this really the case if the matter be rightly understood. This declaration, however, having been once authoritatively pronounced, and the Legislature pertinaciously denying, or at least delaying, any measure of reconciliation, the Church of Scotland has been left no alternative but to determine, whether she would give up herself, or her established connection with the State. . . . The Church has, under existing circumstances, found herself compelled to adopt the latter course. Her course on the 18th May 1843, was in execution of the bidding of her conscience, which she has obeyed, and, in doing so, has made heavy sacrifices. Scotland's people and Scotland's strength are with the Church of its ancestors and martyrs."

To all these testimonies should be added that of the missionaries to Jew and Gentile, who unanimously cast in their lot with the Free Church.

There was no new Act of the Legislature in 1843, as there had been in 1662, when, by express Statute, all ecclesiastical jurisdiction was abolished. In 1662, all Acts of Parliament by which the sole and only power and jurisdiction within this Church doth stand in the Church, are annulled, and the jurisdiction is transferred to the State, or rather to the king as supreme. But while no similar Act was passed in 1843, the Church, then established, became subject to the same servitude as had been imposed in 1662. It became so, not by Act of Parliament, but by judgments of the Civil Courts, whereby all jurisdiction in the Church was swept away. It was an easy and quiet way of effecting a revolution, and yet it was very real and determinate, for the refusal of the Legislature to interfere and to defend the guaranteed liberties of the Church, rested on the assumption that whatever the Civil Courts asserted to be within their province was really so, and that Church Courts were under subjection to their judgments without limitation. Both parties in the State held that any separate and supreme jurisdiction in the Church was intolerable, and that in Scotland there should not be, as Melville had asserted, two kings and two kingdoms. They ignored the Acts of Parliament, recognising and confirming ecclesiastical jurisdiction, and virtually, if not in express terms, entirely annulled all such jurisdiction. And the Church, which was then established, was subject to this condition. In the course of the discussions, indeed, which terminated in the Disruption, Dr. Cook had said—"No language employed in asserting the spiritual independence of the Church, and claiming the powers which it has received from its great Head, could be stronger than I should willingly adopt." And again: "Were any power to attempt to wrest our sacred privileges from us, we should march out together to defend them, displaying the banner of our great King, and determined, could we not gain the victory, to perish in the warfare." But all this brave speaking is rendered nugatory by what he also said, "The moment that an Act is declared by the highest judicial authority to be beyond the province of the Church Courts, as by law established, that Act ought to be regarded as illegal, and cannot, consistently with the fundamental principles of all good government, be persisted in." If this be so, of course there *can* be no conflict, and the banner of the great King can never be unfurled.

But was it really so, that all ecclesiastical jurisdiction had been clean swept away, and that the Church now established in Scotland is subordinate in all things to the State? In answering this question, we might advert to the various cases cited in the Claim of Right, and in the Protest, in all of which the decisions of the Court of Session had become law, by the refusal of the Legislature to interpose for the protection of the Church. To do this, however, would lead us into a statement too protracted, and which might be rather perplexing than edifying. I shall content myself, therefore, with particularising three of them, because these are sufficient to indicate how entirely the Established Church has been deprived of the jurisdiction which the Church of Scotland possessed and exercised; and because in these cases the remanent Establishment homologated by its own act the jurisdiction assumed by the State through the agency of the Civil Courts.

In the first place, it was bound under the new law to intrude ministers upon reclaiming congregations, in violation of the discipline of the Church, as hitherto recognised and declared. The Church, indeed, had often, under the reign of Moderatism, wickedly intruded ministers, in spite of her own laws to the contrary; but now for the first time the Established Church came under obligation to the State to perpetrate this iniquity, thereby separating herself from the law and discipline of the Church of Scotland. Contrary to the law of the Church, and in obedience to the decisions of the Civil Courts, ministers were intruded at Marnoch and Auchterarder against the will of the large congregations in both places—the intruders justifying themselves on the ground that they were thereby obeying the law of the land. They did not even deem it necessary to rescind the Act on Calls, but regarded it as a nullity. Nor, so far as the Established Church is concerned, was this state of things altered by subsequent legislation. The Act of Lord Aberdeen still left it under the obligation to intrude; but the Act abolishing Patronage has since been passed, under which intrusions are no longer possible. But the Established Church has admitted and acted on the principle that she is subject to the State in either case. When she was bidden to intrude she did it on the avowed principle of her subjection to the State, and this subjection has not been altered by the Act abolishing Patronage. It is by order of the State that she still regulates the settlements of ministers, and, if patronage were restored, would doubtless again intrude them.

In the second place, the Established Church has recognised the right of the Civil Court to determine the validity of the deposition of ministers, and, notwithstanding such deposition, not only to secure to them the fruits of the benefice, but to retain them in the office and functions of the ministry. In 1842 seven ministers in the Presbytery of Strathbogie were deposed by the General Assembly, under a libel charging them with various offences. These offences, being violations of the jurisdiction of the Church, were perhaps rather regarded as a merit by the Civil Court, and their deposition was declared to be invalid, and of no effect. So far the Civil Court was doubtless entitled to look into the grounds of the deposition, and, if they found it contrary to law, to secure that it should not have the effect of depriving the ministers of the fruits of the benefice. But the Court went a great deal further than this. They found that these ministers still retained their office, and, although deposed, were notwithstanding ministers of the Established Church. And this finding was acquiesced in by the Assembly which met immediately after the Disruption. These ministers were not reponed by any Act of the Church. Their deposition was simply ignored, and they were recognised as ministers by decree of the Court of Session. Thus the Established Church homologated an Act which strikes at the root of all ecclesiastical jurisdiction; and all Acts of discipline on the part of the Church, whether in the case of office-bearers, or of members, are liable to be subverted by the decision of a Civil Court. But the Established Church has not only tacitly, but by her own Act, subjected herself to this rule, and has thus surrendered all those liberties which had been secured to the Church of Scotland by many hard and protracted conflicts.

In the third place, in 1834, the General Assembly passed an Act, whereby ministers of Chapels of Ease, as they were called, were admitted members of Church Courts, and were authorised to organise Kirk-Sessions, and to carry on the administration of their congregations as other ministers of the Church did. They had also districts assigned to them, which were parishes *quoad sacra*, and in these they were authorised to carry on the ordinary work of evangelisation for the good of the people within the territory assigned to them by the Presbytery. The position of these ministers previously had been altogether anomalous and unpresbyterian, and this was due to the predominance of Moderatism, which discouraged the erection of churches outside the old parochial system; and the ministers of such churches occupied simply the position of ordained preachers. Such a state of things was intolerable in a reforming Presbyterian Church, whose aim was to do what it could to supply the ever-increasing spiritual destitution existing in many quarters of the land. The new order of things at once led to a great increase in the number of congregations, and in the agencies for reclaiming to Christian observances the lapsed population. In the course of a very few years about two hundred congregations were added to the Church, and the movement was earnestly supported by all classes of the community. The old parishes meanwhile remained untouched *quoad civilia.* Stipends, churches, manses, and glebes, all property and perquisites, belonging to the parish ministers remained as they were. The provision attempted, and actually made, was for the spiritual wants of the people, and the measures adopted for this end were those which the Church had experienced to be most effectual. The new churches were built, and their ministers and other agents were maintained, entirely by voluntary liberality. But this movement, so promising and prosperous, was at once arrested by the interference of the Civil Court, at the instance of heritors of Stewarton parish. The Court found that ministers of these parishes *quoad sacra* had no legal place in Church Courts, and were not legally entitled to have Kirk-Sessions. This made the Disruption in 1843 inevitable, unless the Church was prepared to deprive these ministers and their elders of their proper functions as church rulers, for many of the elected members of the Assembly of that year were interdicted, in consequence of the decision in the Stewarton case, from sitting and voting. The remanent Assembly yielded a prompt obedience to that decision, as indeed they were prepared to yield obedience to any decision given by such authority. Accordingly such ministers of *quoad sacra* churches as remained in the Establishment were at once stripped of their function as church rulers, and their Kirk-Sessions ceased to exist. And, under this rule, the Established Church still acts, recognising the right of Civil Courts to determine what functions ministers shall be entitled to exercise, and the right to deprive them of the functions with which they had been invested by the Church. In the case of Strathbogie, the Established Church has yielded to the Civil Court the right of those ministers to remain ministers, whom the Church had deprived of the office. In this case they have yielded the right of depriving of their office ministers whom the Church had invested with it. Thus on both sides the essential jurisdiction of the Church has been trampled under foot, and the Establishment consents to occupy this humiliating position. Since 1843, indeed, facilities have been by Act of Parliament opened up for the erection of new parishes. But unless such parishes are erected in terms of law, their ministers in the Established Church occupy the same position as the Stewarton case placed them in. They are simply ordained preachers, having no power or function of rule and discipline.

LECTURE VI.

RELATION OF CHURCH AND STATE IN SCOTLAND (*continued*).

THE relation to the State of the Established Church in Scotland is one of entire subjection of the Church to the State—a subjection all the more scandalous and intolerable, in that it is the extremest departure from the relation previously existing—a departure not the less real that it has been effected, not by any Act of the Legislature, but by the assumption that the Church of Scotland never had any distinct and independent jurisdiction. It was different in 1662 and 1669, when the State assumed, in the person of the king, the absolute control over the Church. It was then openly avowed that the State deprived the Church of what it had formerly possessed. The Act 1662 annulled "all Acts of Parliament by which the sole and only power and jurisdiction within this Church doth stand in the Church, and in the General, Provincial and Presbyterial Assemblies and Kirk-Sessions;" and in the Act 1669 "it is declared that his majesty hath the supreme authority and supremacy over all persons, and in all causes ecclesiastical, within his kingdom; and that, by virtue thereof, the ordering and disposal of the external government and policy of the Church doth properly belong to his majesty and his successors as an inherent right to the Crown."

Nothing can be clearer than that the right thus transferred to the king was a right previously possessed by the Church. But these acts of usurpation having been entirely swept away in 1690, the Church assumed the exercise of her former jurisdiction and liberties, which were secured to her so far as legislation could, and by the subsequent Act of Security were placed beyond the power of the British Parliament. Notwithstanding, in 1843, these liberties were assumed to be non-existent. Such being the relation of the Scottish Establishment to the State, the Free Church cannot but earnestly desire that this relation should be dissolved. It is a relation formed not only in violation of solemn treaties, but which in its nature involves sin, both on the part of those who have subjected the Church to bondage, and on the part of those who submit to the yoke. By abandoning her connection with the State rather than submit to it, the Free Church has declared, in the most emphatic way, that it is better to have no Established Church than an Establishment subjected to Erastian control. The fathers of the Free Church, indeed, formed a very high estimate—we may say a very exaggerated estimate—of the value and importance of State Establishment and Endowment; but they attached an unspeakably higher value to the freedom of the Church to conform to the will of Christ, as they read it in His Word. It might reasonably enough have been expected, in these circumstances, that the Free Church would have continuously and earnestly endeavoured to procure the dissolution of the existing relation between Church and State in Scotland. That it has not done so may be easily accounted for without implying any dereliction of duty.

1. The Free Church, by her representation and appeal to the Legislature in her Claim of Right in

1842, and by her own action at the Disruption in 1843, had very fully discharged the duty laid upon her in this respect. She could not more clearly enforce her claim than she had done in 1842; and she could not in a more expressive way declare her condemnation of the existing relation between Church and State than by her exodus in 1843. She would only have weakened her cause by a repetition of her claim addressed to those who had already, in no doubtful terms, rejected it, and who showed no indications of a change of sentiment. It might have been different if her claim had been rejected by one only of the great parties in the State. But it was repudiated alike by both parties; and her conduct as a Free Church was continually, although indirectly, bearing witness to the wrong that had been done her, and calling upon the Legislature to redress it.

2. Her Claim of Right plainly enough indicated that it was not her purpose to continue an agitation to have it recognised and sanctioned. She did not indeed finally abandon it, but reserved to those who made the claim, or to their successors, the freedom "at any time hereafter,

when there shall be a prospect of obtaining justice, to claim the restitution of all such civil rights and privileges, and temporal benefits and endowments, as for the present they may be compelled to yield up." She did not recognise the pressing of the claim as an urgent and immediate duty. She did not even seek to impose it upon the Church as a duty at any future time. The freedom to renew the claim was simply reserved. She did not, on the rejection of her claim, abandon it finally, but neither did she contemplate the obligation of pressing it unseasonably upon the Legislature. She was content to abide the time "when there shall be a prospect of obtaining justice," leaving it to the wisdom and discretion of those who succeeded to determine when such a time should arrive. That time, we may surely say, has not yet arrived. The Legislature of to-day is certainly not more disposed to render justice to the Free Church than that of a past generation. And circumstances may arise, I believe they have arisen, which render it to the last degree improbable that the time will ever come when it will be the duty of the Free Church to press this claim. To do this is, and must always be, a matter, not of obligation, but of Christian wisdom, and subordinate to the higher ends for which the Church exists and operates.

3. This fact doubtless was largely influential in determining the Free Church not to prosecute her rightful claim during the years immediately succeeding the Disruption. She had higher and more sacred work to do than to be knocking at the door of Parliament, and wasting her energies in a hopeless quest. She had to supply the means of grace to the many thousands who were earnestly seeking her ministrations. She had to provide a maintenance for the five hundred ministers who, at the bidding of conscience, and in the service of their Great Master, had given up all that they had in the world. She had to build churches for their houseless congregations, and dwellings for the ministers themselves; besides affording the same sustenance and accommodation to numerous congregations who, apart from their ministers, became members of her communion. She had to vindicate her claim to be the true Church of Scotland, by extending her ministrations to the remotest corners of the land, so that no one who desired to receive

ordinances at her hands should be excluded from the privilege. She had, besides, to prosecute the great enterprises on which, through the spirit of grace poured out upon her, she had entered previous to the Disruption,—at home, to repair the waste-places of many generations within the realm of Scotland ; and abroad, to the extent of her capabilities, to fulfil the great commission to preach the Gospel to every creature. All this was her proper work, both as a Church of Christ and as the Church of Scotland ; and by the grace of God she has been enabled in some measure, notwithstanding many sins and shortcomings, to fulfil her ministry. She has abandoned no enterprise undertaken when she was an Established Church. On the contrary, she has prosecuted them all on an enlarged and ever-increasing scale, besides entering upon new fields of labour. Can there be any doubt that, if she had bent her energies to seeking restitution of her temporal benefits, she would have weakened her hands, and come down from her great work to engage in a conflict far less sacred, and unspeakably less important ?

4. If the Free Church had been so unwise as

to follow such a course, her character in the face of the world could not fail to have been compromised. It was right that she should protest against the injustice done to her—right also to show that she had a just claim for restitution; but having done this, it behoved her to take joyfully the spoiling of her goods, and in her new position to bend her undivided energies to accomplish her great aims as a Church of Christ. It was thus only that she could maintain her character as a Church. If the State, notwithstanding her protest, withheld its aid, the responsibility lay upon it; and she must show that she could live and do her proper work apart from it, as she had done in the earlier years of her history. It would both have crippled her energies and stained her character to turn aside, and vainly endeavour to get restored what had been unrighteously taken away.

It has been represented, indeed, that Establishment is one of the principles of the Free Church. If it were so, then, by relinquishing the Establishment, she must be held as having abandoned one of her principles. The Church of Scotland never denied that it was the right and duty of the State, in certain circumstances, to establish and endow the Church. But that was a matter external to herself, and did not concern her principles or administration. She organised herself, and administered her affairs apart from the State, and independently of it, for several years before she was acknowledged by the State, and her establishment and endowment in no way affected her internal government. Her concern was that, whether Established or not, her jurisdiction should remain intact; and that she should, in either case, be free to regulate her affairs under responsibility to Him whom she acknowledged as her sole King and Head. It was for the State to determine whether it was its duty to establish and endow her. The Church believed and said that such was its duty. But her establishment was an accident in her history, and not a principle in her administration. In her earliest years she did just what the Free Church is now doing. Having no State aid, she relied upon the free-will offerings of her members, just as the Church had done for three hundred years at the commencement of the Christian era. And in these last days God has given her more abundant cause to trust and not be afraid, that all temporal things will be freely and lovingly given to her, if she is found faithful in doing the work assigned to her by her gracious Lord. She cannot but desire that the existing relation between Church and State in Scotland should be dissolved—a relation of sinful subserviency which is neither glorifying to God nor conducive to the highest well-being of men.

If this consummation were realised, it is hardly conceivable that the question could be raised as to the establishment and endowment of another Church; and least of all on the basis of the Claim of Right of the Free Church. What it might be the right and duty of the State to do in certain conditions of society—such, for instance, as when there was only one Church organisation, and when the community were of one mind on the matter—it might be inconsistent with the principles of common equity, and therefore injurious to religion, to do when these conditions of society were reversed. And this is the state of things in Scotland now. A great and ever-growing change has been in progress since 1843; and what it might have been right to do then, it might be wrong to do at present. The wrong which was done then cannot be remedied now; and the time has passed away when the Free Church could legitimately, either in her own interests or in the interests of Catholic Christianity, seek restitution of her temporal benefits and endowments. The seeking of such restitution was not regarded in 1842, and in terms of the Claim of Right, as obligatory. The Church was simply declared free to do this in more favourable circumstances, which have not emerged, and are less likely to emerge, in the future. The Free Church therefore abandons no principle in refraining from the prosecution of this claim, or even in finally relinquishing it. In thus acting, she parts with nothing that inherently belongs to her as a Church of Christ; she retains her creed, her worship, her discipline and government, and her freedom of jurisdiction. Moreover, she gives additional emphasis to her Protest, that the conditions of the present Establishment are "contrary to and subversive of the settlement of Church Government effected at the Revolution, and solemnly guaranteed by the Act of Security and Treaty of Union; are also at variance with God's Word, in opposition to the doctrines and fundamental principles of the Church of Scotland, inconsistent with the freedom essential to the right constitution of a Church of Christ, and incompatible with the government which He, as the Head of His Church, hath therein appointed distinct from the civil magistrate."

Surely the Free Church cannot but earnestly desire, if she is true to her principles, that an institution so conditioned should not be maintained. Whether, if the existing relation between Church and State were dissolved, another Establishment on a purer basis, recognising and confirming the freedom and independent jurisdiction of the Church, could or should be set up,—is a question which cannot be regarded as coming within the range of practical administration. Considering the character and views of the Legislature, and the divided state of religious sentiment in the community, the setting up of another Establishment is an enterprise that no wise man would attempt, and no Christian should aim at who has a supreme regard to the interests of religion. And even were circumstances more favourable, it is difficult to conceive how an Establishment could be constituted with more stringent securities for the independent jurisdiction of the Church than were possessed by the Church of Scotland; and yet they were all trampled upon and set at nought, and what has been done in the past may be done again in the future.

Surely the Church of Scotland had very good ground for believing that, as established, she was left free to act upon her convictions of what the will of Christ required, on the lines of her own recognised constitution. These grounds of belief have been frequently and forcibly set forth, and it is unnecessary to repeat them in detail. But, in order to a clear understanding of the principles of the Free Church, it is of importance that they should be exhibited in their historical setting. And this I shall endeavour to do as briefly as is consistent with making them intelligible.

Among the churches of the Reformation the Church of Scotland held a position which was quite unique. This was partly due, doubtless, to the fact that the State took nothing to do with its formation; but much more to the fact that God had raised up at least one man of singular endowments to take the leading part in organising the Reformed Church. In these days in which we live historians and statesmen are more and more intelligently recognising how much Scotland owes to John Knox—how much Europe and the cause of the Reformation owe to him. By his natural endowments, and by large experience and full information, he was peculiarly qualified for taking the part he did in the Scottish Reformation. Possessed of a courage insensible to fear, and pure-hearted in his devotion to divine truth, as it was known to him, he was not subject to those influences by which so many have been turned aside from the straight path of rectitude. He and a few others, in whose hearts was shining the light of the knowledge of the glory of God in the face of Jesus Christ, were drawn together by that impulse which moves all Christian souls to consider what they ought to do. They recognised it as the will of Christ that they should be organised into a body, and with the open Bible in their hands, and looking for and expecting the guidance of the Divine Spirit, they set themselves to determine, as the Lord might lead them, what form the organised body should assume, and what functions belong respectively to its office-bearers and its members. They asked for and received in this matter no counsel or direction from the State. It was a matter which belonged exclusively to them as the servants of Christ to determine in the light of God's word, framing all things according to the pattern, as they were able to decipher it, delineated in the Scriptures. Accordingly, they set about framing a Book of Discipline, without counsel or direction from the State. By an Act of Parliament (1560), indeed, the Papal jurisdiction was abolished, but no other was set up in its stead. What was done in reference to religion was done by the Church alone. With a view to future legislation the Privy Council granted a commission to five ministers to frame rules for ecclesiastical government, and these completed their task in May 1560, and presented the result of their labours in the form of the First Book of Discipline, which was afterwards adopted by the General Assembly, and was subscribed by very many of the nobility and gentry. This book is in many ways a very remarkable production, and had great influence in shaping the future history of Scotland. Besides what relates to the ecclesiastical discipline and policy of the Church it contains a brief confession of faith, and proposals for national education, so wise and comprehensive, that to this day we are only aiming at the entire completion of the scheme.

It would be beside our present purpose, however, to detail its several provisions,—only this may be noted in regard to the appointment of ministers that this principle is announced: "It appertaineth to the people, and to every several congregation, to elect their minister."

Some twenty years afterwards, a second Book of Discipline was prepared, and was adopted by the General Assembly, 1581. This book did not supersede or abrogate that which had been previously adopted, but was rendered necessary by the progress which had been made in the plantation of churches over the different provinces of the kingdom, and thus putting the Church in a position in which was required a more specific determination of various matters of order for the regulation of her procedure.

This book, like the first, was entirely the work of the Church, prepared and adopted without the concurrence or direction of the State. From first to last, indeed, the whole organisation of the Church was determined by the Church herself, acting independently, and exercising the functions which she believed to be inherent in a church of Christ, and under the guidance of His revealed will. Neither of the books was adopted or confirmed in its entireness by the State, but they were, and continued to be, the rule for the administration of the Church, and for the exercise of her discipline and government.

Among the provisions of the "Second Book of Discipline," I may quote the following as bearing upon the subject of these lectures:—"The power and policy ecclesiastical is different and distinct in its own nature from that power and policy which is called the Civil Power, and appertains to the civil government of the commonwealth; albeit they be both of God and tend to one end, if they be rightly used, namely, to advance the glory of God, and to have godly and good subjects. For the power ecclesiastical flows immediately from God and the Mediator Jesus

Christ, and is spiritual, not having a temporal head on earth, but only Christ, the only spiritual King and Governor of His kirk. The magistrate ought to assist, maintain, and fortify the jurisdiction of the kirk. The ministers should assist their princes in all things agreeable to the Word, providing they neglect not their own charge by involving themselves in civil affairs." So much as to the relation of Church and State. Then as to the appointment of office-bearers in the Church, the book says: "Election is the choosing out of a person or persons most able to the office that is vacant, by the judgment of the eldership and consent of the congregation, to whom the person or persons are appointed. In this ordinary election it is to be eschewed that no person be intruded in any of the offices of the kirk contrary to the will of the congregation to whom they are appointed, or without the voice of the eldership." In harmony moreover with the declaration of the "First Book of Discipline," this book declares: "The liberty of election of persons called to the ecclesiastical functions, and observed without interruption so long as the kirk was not corrupted by Antichrist, we desire to be restored and retained within this realm." And it is added, "This order, which God's Word craves, cannot stand with patronages and presentation to benefices used in the pope's kirk."

Fifteen General Assemblies had been held before the Reformed Church received any recognition from the State. In these assemblies all the ordinary functions of church government and discipline were discharged, in the plantation of kirks and the settlement or removal of ministers—in the exercise of that power which was recognised as inherent in the Church and derived from Divine authority. And in 1567, when the State at length interposed, it was not to the effect of usurping any control over the proper jurisdiction of the Church, but simply to recognise its existence and authority: "The present parliament pronounce and declare that the ministers of the blessed Evangel of Jesus Christ whom God in His mercy has now raised up among us, or hereafter shall, agreeing with them that now live in doctrine and administration of the sacraments, and that part of the people of this realm that professes Jesus Christ as now He is offered in His Evangel, and do communicate with His holy sacraments (as in our reformed kirks they are publicly ministered) may be declared the only true kirk of Jesus Christ within this realm."

It is not necessary to detail the conflict which almost immediately followed, in which the supremacy of the Crown was asserted, and a Prelatic Church was attempted to be set up; for the tyrannical proceedings of that period had no enduring place in the constitution of either Church or State. A counter revolution, which proved successful, ended in the famous Act of Parliament (1592), which has been rightly characterised as the Charter of the Presbyterian Church of Scotland. That Act ratifies and approves General Assemblies, Synods, Presbyteries, and Kirk-Sessions. It declares further, that the Acts 1584 shall in "no wise be prejudicial, nor derogate anything to the privilege that God has given to the spiritual office-bearers in the kirk, concerning heads of religion, matters of heresy, excommunication, collation, or deprivation of ministers, or any such like essential censures, specially grounded and having warrant of the Word of God." Presentations to benefices are finally ordained to be directed to particular presbyteries in all time coming, with full power to give collation thereupon, and to put order to all matters and causes ecclesiastical within their bounds, according to the discipline of the kirk, providing the foresaid presbyteries be bound and astricted to receive and admit whatsoever qualified minister be presented by his majesty or lay patrons. Further, in an Act passed two years later, it is declared that in the event of presbyteries refusing admission to qualified presentees, the patron is to retain the whole fruits of the benefice in his own hand. Such was the legislation in Church and State in Scotland at the end of the sixteenth century. The Church, in the exercise of its self-government, divinely sanctioned, had framed and issued its Confession of Faith, had organised its government by Kirk-Sessions, Presbyteries, Synods, and General Assemblies—had settled the nature and functions of its office-bearers, and prescribed rules for the administration of its affairs. The State, on the other hand, had ratified the government and discipline of the Church, and had expressly recognised its powers as God-given. This state of things was unique among the nations, but it was eminently satisfactory.

During the following century many changes took place, which our limits do not permit us to describe. Nor, for our purpose is it necessary, for at the close of the seventeenth century the relations between Church and State resumed the same position as they held in 1592. Patronage, which had been abolished by the Revolution Settlement, was restored in 1712, for the most nefarious purposes, and in violation of the most solemn obligations; but its restoration did not alter the state of things as they existed in 1592. Till the present century indeed there are only two changes, which affect the legislation of the sixteenth century, and which was the law for Church and State till 1839. The one change was on the part of the State providing that the fruits of the benefice should revert, not to the patron, but to the Ministers' Widows' Fund, in the event of a presbytery refusing to admit a qualified presentee. The other change was on the part of the Church, which, by adopting the Westminster Confession of Faith declared that "the Lord Jesus, as King and Head of His

Church, hath therein appointed a government in the hands of church-officers distinct from the Civil Magistrate"—a declaration confirmatory of the powers God had given to the Church, and which were ratified by the State.

As might reasonably enough have been expected, questions sometimes arose in which the intervention of the Civil Courts was solicited in reference to the settlement of ministers. I can only refer to one of these cases, namely, that of Dunse in 1749. It is reported by Lord Monboddo, who informs us that the Court was asked to discharge the Presbytery from moderating in a call at large, or settling any other man than the presentee. The Court refused to do this, "because that was interfering with the power of ordination, or the internal policy of the Church, with which the Lords thought they had nothing to do." In reference to this matter it is worth while to quote the statement of Lord Kames, though it has been often adverted to, in one of his law tracts on the jurisdiction of Courts. He says—"Ecclesiastical Courts have an important jurisdiction in providing parishes with proper ministers or pastors; and they exercise this jurisdiction by naming for the minister of the vacant church that person, duly qualified, who is presented by the patron. Their sentence is ultimate, even when their proceedings are illegal. The person authorised by their sentence, even in opposition to the presentee, is *de facto* minister of the parish, and as such is entitled to perform every ministerial function; but, though minister of the parish, he has no claim to the stipend." "This check," he adds, "is extremely mild, and yet it is fully effectual to prevent abuse." If this doctrine had been observed there would have been no conflict of jurisdiction in the Auchterarder Case, and possibly no Disruption.

So stood the matter in the relation between Church and State, when the General Assembly, in 1834, enacted what was called the Veto Law. Its purpose was, as I have already stated, to prevent the intrusion of unacceptable ministers; and it provided that a dissent by a majority of male heads of families, being communicants, should be a bar against any further proceedings towards the settlement of a presentee. This law was in several respects defective, and, in conformity with the Book of Discipline, might have been made much more stringent. It might, as a condition of the settlement of a minister, have given the right of dissent to all members of the congregation; or it might have required a positive call from the congregation, instead of recognising their right of veto. And this latter course would have been more in conformity with the then existing regulations of the Church; for it should be borne in mind that the uniform practice of the Church was, that a Presbytery, so soon as they had sustained a presentation, sent the presentee to the congregation, that they might have proof of his gifts to edification; and afterwards proceeded to moderate in a call to him. This practice never ceased to be observed, even during the dominant sway of Moderatism. But while the form was preserved, and was a memorial of better days, its meaning was evacuated. The presentee was settled, whether the congregation called him or not, and their views and feelings were utterly disregarded. But this was a scandalous abuse of ecclesiastical power. Doubtless the law of the Church required that presentees should be settled on the suit and calling of the congregation. The General Assembly adopted the Veto Act as imposing the least possible restriction upon the power of patrons, if the fundamental law against intrusion was to be carried into effect. Perhaps also they were partly led to adopt this course by the legislation of 1649.

The Court of Session, when appealed to, by a majority found this Act illegal. There is no very great presumption in saying that this was an erroneous judgment; but it was a judgment entirely within the competency of the Court, to whom it belonged to interpret and apply the Statutes of the Realm in civil matters. And the Church had no hesitation in coming to the conclusion that, if they proceeded to the settlement of a minister on the rejection of a presentee by a majority of the heads of families, such minister would have no title to the benefice. But on a second application the Court proceeded further, and assumed the right, in the face of law and precedent, to constrain the Presbytery to proceed towards the ordination and induction of the rejected presentee. The Presbytery refused compliance, which indeed they could not yield without violating the principles laid down in their Book of Discipline, and, as they believed, without violating their obligation to the great Head of the Church, who had not made them lords over God's heritage. They believed that they had the law of the State as well as the law of God on their side, for the State had provided the loss of the benefice as the only penalty for the illegal settlement of a minister, or for rejecting a presentee illegally; and therefore they appealed to the Legislature in the Claim of Right. But the procedure of the Court raised and brought into prominence a far higher question, as to the inherent liberties and Divine obligations of the Church. She was under law to a higher Master than any Civil Court, or any State enactment, and was not at liberty to do as she was enjoined. She was bound to obey God rather than man, and her Lord had not left her free to intrude ministers upon reclaiming congregations. This judgment of the Law Courts, upheld and confirmed as it was by the Legislature in rejecting the claim of the Church, made it impossible to remain in a Church established under conditions which separated it from the most cherished traditions and laws of the Reformed Church of Scotland. And even if it had stood alone, it would have necessitated the Disruption which took place in 1843, when a majority of the members, properly constituting the General Assembly of that year, constituted a separate Assembly, which was the lineal representative of the Church of the Reformation, and the maintainer of the vital principles which through all changes of fortune she had asserted and vindicated.

But this was not all. The Civil Court having once invaded the ecclesiastical province, and assumed the right of dealing with the Church as its servant, in the matter of ordaining and inducting ministers, could not well stop short at that point, as one of their own number had significantly warned them. They were very soon called upon to interpose with equal effect in the matter of the deposition of ministers. In order to prevent the intrusion of a minister at New Marnoch, which the presbytery of Strathbogie had declared it to be their intention to do, the Supreme Court of the Church suspended seven of the ministers of that presbytery from their functions, that they might be hindered from perpetrating such an outrage. These seven ministers applied to the Court of Session to remove this sentence of suspension, and the Court granted their application, and relieved them from the sentence of suspension. And acting upon this, these ministers resumed their functions and carried into effect their shameful work of intrusion. The subsequent General Assembly deposed these ministers from their office, under a libel containing eight distinct charges grounded on the general proposition that the Lord Jesus Christ had instituted a government in His Church, in the hands of church officers, distinct from the Civil Magistrate; that the infliction and removal of church censures are inherently parts of that government; that every minister vows obedience and engages to maintain and defend that government; that it is contrary to God's Word and the laws and constitution of this Church for any office-bearers therein to seek in any way by the Civil power to exempt and withdraw themselves from the jurisdiction of the Church. In his speech for sustaining the libel, Dr. Cunningham, after having shown that these ministers had broken the laws of the Church and violated their ordination vow, said, "These would of themselves have afforded adequate grounds for depriving them of their status and privileges as ministers of the Church of Scotland. But I would not think it right, on the great scriptural principles which ought to regulate the exercise of ecclesiastical discipline, to depose men from the office of the holy ministry in Christ's Church unless we could prove that these men have been guilty of a sin against Him who is King and Head of the Church. Their voluntary administration of ordinances, when under suspension, falls under the same head as their voluntary application to the Civil Court to suspend our sentences, and to restore them to their functions. Now this latter step is plainly a renunciation of the allegiance they owed to the Lord Jesus Christ, as the only King and Head of His Church; it is plainly a denial of His sole Headship and supremacy, and of the truth contained in the Confession of Faith, and ratified by the law of the land, that Jesus Christ is King and Head of His Church, and that He has appointed therein a government in the hands of church officers distinct from the Civil magistrate. It plainly involves a denial of the position that to His office-bearers, and to them alone, are committed the keys. The truth is that these men have already virtually pronounced a sentence of deposition upon themselves. The sum and substance of what is implied in the acts charged upon them is, that they have virtually renounced their allegiance to Christ as the only King and Head of the Church, and enrolled themselves as the servants of another master."

As a matter of course the sentence of deposition was revoked by the Court of Session, and these ministers, having no other authority for discharging the functions of the ministerial office than that of the Civil Court, continued to act as if they had never been deposed, and the sentence of the General Assembly was never recalled.

But even this was not enough. As if it had been necessary to make manifest how entire was the usurpation by the civil power of the proper jurisdiction of the Church, the Court interposed by interdict in arresting the proceedings of the Church in almost all matters of Church discipline, even to the extent of prohibiting the preaching of the Gospel in certain localities. Whatever they were asked to do in this way, in fact they did, and their usurpation, the Legislature refused to redress, and therefore confirmed as a condition of the Established Church. As they had interfered to the effect of compelling presbyteries, under penalties, to take steps towards intruding presentees upon reclaiming congregations—as they still further interfered to find invalid a sentence of deposition, they completed the round of usurpation by interfering to compel the Church to deprive ministers of their functions as church rulers. I have already adverted to this last act of usurpation, and need not now repeat what was done, nor advert to the compulsitor which still rests upon the Church established by law in Scotland.

If, therefore, the Church of Scotland was to exist as established after the Reformation; if it was to retain the fundamental principles of its Books of Discipline; if it was to have a government distinct from the civil magistrate—it was imperatively necessary to separate from the State, and to surrender all the emoluments conferred by the State, and to assert its freedom from State control, and its obligation to serve Christ as its only King and Head.

This was the position taken by the true Church of Scotland in 1843, and ever since maintained by the Free Church. It is a position which brings her into very close relationship with her living Head, which lays her under very special obligations to be observant of and submissive to His will in all things, and to act under a sense of her dependence on Him. And so long as she is faithful to this profession, and walks according to His direction in humble and devoted obedience to His will, she may expect that the blessing of the Lord will rest upon her, that His power will attend her ministrations, and that she will be kept pure in doctrine. In all her past history it has been found true that her time of enlargement has been coincident with her assertion of the lordship of Christ. It was so in a very marked way, in the last generation, and will be so in time to come, if she be found faithful—if her office-bearers and members, realising what is implied in the faith they profess, shall continue to live under His guidance, and humbly follow it, feeling their indebtedness to Him for all that they are and have, and their obligation to serve Him who is their Lord and their God, who has redeemed them by His blood and made them His freed men.

Printed by Frank Murray, *9 & 11 Young Street, Edinburgh.*